Good l  g

Good Morning

Joseph Stevens

Grand Valley State University
Allendale, Michigan

GRAND VALLEY
STATE UNIVERSITY

EDITOR: ROBERT FRANCIOSI
PROJECT COORDINATOR: ROGER GILLES
BOOK DESIGN AND ELECTRONIC PAGE MAKEUP: DAN ROYER
PRINTER: CUSTOM PRINTERS, GRAND RAPIDS, MI

PUBLISHED BY GRAND VALLEY STATE UNIVERSITY
Good Morning by Joseph Stevens

Cover Photo: Left to right, Janek and Tolek Jankowski
with "Szczupak," (Joseph Stevens) c. 1942

ISBN: 0-9709811-0-4

*For Jack and Rick, who wanted to
know about my past.*

Joseph Stevens
Freedom Endowment
≈⥿

Grand Valley State University established the Joseph Stevens Freedom Endowment to honor the long-time Grand Rapids resident and Holocaust survivor. Stevens has shared his story with numerous GVSU students, bringing history to the classroom and reminding us all how easily people can destroy each other by forgetting history's lessons.

The endowment funds the Joseph Stevens Lecture Series, which brings speakers to GVSU and Grand Rapids who promote an understanding of the problems and issues associated with the struggle for human freedom. Whenever possible, the lectures will focus on the Nazi genocide and on the consequences of racial prejudice.

All proceeds from the sale of this book support the Joseph Stevens Freedom Endowment.

ACKNOWLEDGMENTS

‿ↄↄ

Good Morning's path to publication has been a winding one. As Professor William Baum recounts in his preface, Joseph Stevens began to tell his story during the 1980s, first to college students, then to other West Michigan audiences. Eventually, these talks inspired Grand Rapids city historian, Gordon Olson, to conduct an oral history interview with him. A transcript of that tape served Stevens as a starting point for his written memoirs, a version prompted by his sons, Jack and Rick.

Last year Hank Meijer brought an initial draft to the attention of President Arend D. Lubbers of Grand Valley State University, and the essential support of these two men, as well as that of Frederik Meijer, has enabled the publication of *Good Morning.*

Members of the GVSU English Department have participated in the following ways: Roger Gilles coordinated the project, Dan Royer designed the book, and Rob Franciosi organized and edited the manuscript. Finally, Jo Ellyn Clarey made invaluable contributions throughout the editorial process.

"Good morning" is an expression used daily by millions, often without sentiment or sincerity. To me it is a warm greeting very close to my heart. I fell in love with it, and will continue to love it until the end of my days.

There was a time in my life when, upon awakening in the morning, I considered it a blessing to greet someone with "Good morning," to spend another day on this tragic earth. Going to sleep in the evening, I always felt as if I had lived my last day. Waking in the morning, I was always amazed that I was still alive. The surprise gave me the courage, strength, and will power to fight without fear for the Allied cause one more day. Each day, then, was to me the most precious gift. I was sure that I would not come out of the war alive.

Therefore, "Good morning!"

— Joseph Stevens

PREFACE

William Baum

During the sixteen years I have taught courses on the Holocaust at Grand Valley State University, I have frequently been asked how I cope with the horror of it all. My answer normally testifies to the human capacity to do anything to anyone, but I hasten to add that teaching these courses has yielded an unexpected benefit: I have met some most interesting people. One of these is Joe Stevens, who has become a good friend to both my wife and myself. Joe's fascinating story is now in front of you.

Those who already know Joe Stevens describe him as an intelligent, sensitive and kindly man. Those who meet him through this memoir will hasten to add "brilliant" and "tough" to the terms of description. Over the years while hearing Joe tell his story to my classes, I have been intrigued by how much his survival was dependent upon his own striking intelligence.

People who survived the Holocaust often acknowledge how important luck was to surviving their hells on earth. Joe Stevens also mentions an especially difficult situation when he "put all [his] trust in luck." But this is not typical of Joe Stevens and is inconsistent with what else we learn about him. Shining brightest through this remarkable narrative is his shrewd wisdom. Time after time, Joe avoided

Nazi efforts to round up every Jew possible by simply out-
smarting his adversaries. From the beginning Joe refused,
for example, to wear the Star of David, which publicly
and conspicuously identified Jews as targets for destruction. In his own words:

> All Jews were soon required to wear armbands with
> yellow stars, visible to all. The German edict, posted
> everywhere, specified the exact size of the star and
> how it should be worn. . . . The moment I read the
> decree I decided to disobey it. Though the penalty for
> defying the order was death, I realized that wearing
> the star would lead to my end. Why expose myself to
> the additional humiliation?

Why indeed. But as Joe's story so clearly illustrates, his
survival required more than the stubborn refusal to wear
the yellow star—yes, some good luck to be sure; Joe would
admit that. But in his case, an extraordinary intelligence
does most of the work.

Joe is no longer the vigorous young man with a frozen
mustache who dared enter the Jewish ghetto in Vilnius
because, having heard so many gruesome stories, he "simply wanted to know what was going on." Aware that he
was putting his "head in the lion's mouth," Joe acknowl-
edges, "I always did have a tendency toward embarking
upon dangerous ventures." It is now nearly sixty years
later. Members of my current classes, fortunate enough to
hear Joe Stevens tell his story, today meet an elderly man
with white hair who is soft spoken and burdened by the
loss of his family to the Nazi onslaught.

His memories are truly unimaginable for most of us and
were for a long while understandably repressed by Joe
Stevens. Some years ago, however, Joe decided to risk the
assault memory would make on his uneasy calm by writ-

Good Morning

ing his memoirs and telling his story to students. These endeavors have required great effort and resolution, but Joe's decision to share his experience of life during the Holocaust is consistent with his dedication to knowing as much as possible about whatever situation he is in. What could be more important than sharing with students the ugly consequences of extreme arrogance and intolerance. I believe Joe has made a difference to those who listen to and reflect on what he has to say. As the story presented here clearly demonstrates, even one person with intelligence and courage can make a difference.

Here, then, is the survivor of the Holocaust who speaks to my classes whenever possible. Joe used to visit every time the class was offered, but several years ago he began spending the cold months in Israel returning to Grand Rapids only during the warmer seasons. Joe says he feels more comfortable in Israel — more comfortable, I am sure, with many others who share the dark stain of the Holocaust. Nevertheless, Joe still has ties in West Michigan, and his return visits often include presentations to students at Grand Valley.

In 1990, GVSU was pleased to honor Joe by establishing the Joseph Stevens Freedom Fund. The money from this permanent endowment is used to further education about the Holocaust and other inhuman events.

11

INTRODUCTION

❦

Robert Franciosi

In June 1944 when the Nazis had retreated west, Joseph Stevens and his partisan comrades could at last show themselves in the light of day as fighters. They were to parade before their leaders in what should have been Stevens's most gratifying moment. But when a young sergeant assigned him to have his troops build an altar for the ceremony, they traded words. The following exchange captures both the complexities of Stevens's clandestine life between 1940 and 1944 and, perhaps, the secret of his survival:

> Surprised, I opened my eyes and asked, "With what?" He snapped back, "Are you a Jew and don't know how to organize an altar?" I froze for a moment, but knew I had to react, and said angrily, "For such language I should knock your teeth out, but I can't because I respect your uniform." He gave me a dirty look and walked away without saying a word. I was satisfied with my own conduct in the situation; I had acted as a paper tiger.

The young Joseph Stevens had schooling and experience in the printing trade, his family's business in the Polish city of Kalisz. But while the Nazis ruled Eastern Europe he worked at jobs he'd neither trained for nor ever imagined for himself: window glazier, architect's helper, road builder, farmer, fish hatchery worker, occasionally even catechist for the local Catholic church. Readers of this volume might conclude that Stevens missed his real life's calling as an actor. With consummate ability to assume whatever part was necessary to survive, he played many roles during the war, always concealing his Jewishness. The performances recounted here are impressive. Some are enacted by Szczecinski, his birth name; some, by Szczupak, or "pike," his war alias; others, by Joe Stevens, his American name.

Acting a clever part with the young sergeant is just one illustration of Stevens's ability to read a situation quickly and invent the necessary gestures and words for a particular role. His stirring memoir includes so many that we might easily forget the life-and-death stakes involved or not appreciate the often absurd predicaments of Stevens's situation. For several years he lived among Lithuanian and Polish Catholics whose hatred for the Nazis was only equaled by their animosity towards Jews. Even after the Germans left, Józef Szczecinski had to hide his Jewish identity. The audience may have changed, but this masterful actor knew he must stay in character until the war's bitter end.

Decades later, Stevens took on yet another largely unchosen role, one which he no doubt would have gladly foregone: Holocaust witness. Memoir and testimony, of course, have been the signature Holocaust literary forms, the works of professional writers Elie Wiesel, Primo Levi, and Charlotte Delbo among the most enduring. While the urgent need for Holocaust survivors to bear witness has been the point of departure in nearly all discussions of memoirs, the ever-growing list of published volumes seems to ensure that few will have a unique impact. Add to these the thousands of recorded testimonies, and distinguishing one particular account, especially one written by an amateur, from the moving, often shocking, assembly becomes very difficult. Confronted with so many eye-witness testimonies today, experienced readers of these grim chronicles can easily feel a sense of fatigue before even beginning another narrative from Hitler's war against the Jews.

Such weariness describes my first reaction when I was asked to read the manuscript of this book. I knew about Joseph Stevens and his many contributions to Bill Baum's course on the Holocaust at Grand Valley State University. I had even met him in passing, but my knowledge of his particular history was sketchy. In retrospect, I'm glad for my limited knowledge of the story he has regularly shared with college students over the years. Because my contact had been minimal, I've been able not only to "meet" Stevens through this full written treatment, but I've been surprised to learn that his is not a Holocaust story of atrocity, finally, but of human resiliency. What I am terming "resiliency" others might call "toughness," or in Hemingway's terms, "grace under pressure," a quality shared by many trauma survivors. More than sheer courage, resiliency is a characteristic allowing one, at a moment's notice, to process and adjust to changing, often dangerous, circumstances. It names a pattern of engagement with the world.

Describing Stevens's narrative as a story of human resiliency, though, is not to deny the atmosphere of mass death hovering over it; indeed, as he writes, throughout the war he never knew whether a single night's action would be his last. And his account of a visit to the ghetto in Vilnius reveals just what fate awaited him were his Jewish identity discovered. Like the film hero of *Europa, Europa,* another factual tale from a grotesque land in which a young Jew survives by playing the Nazi among Germans and the Communist among Russians, Stevens assumes a chameleon-like stance toward a chaotic and brutal world. Again and again he demonstrates in this memoir how his powers of observation and adaptation were his keys to survival.

How would I react in such desperate circumstances?" is a question most students of the Holocaust inevitably pose to themselves. The casual or inexperienced perhaps too easily assume they would make the heroic, moral choice. Yet if countless performers from the Nazi era teach us anything—be they victims, perpetrators, or bystanders—we know we cannot easily predict our behavior in the face of radical evil. A large number of survivor memoirs suggest, however, that certain individuals unquestionably possessed habits of mind and behavior which at least helped them to survive. Stevens's keen ability to observe, best displayed here in the memorable "Start" pen scene, planted the seeds of his survival. Being ever-watchful, as Stevens was, did not guarantee his fate. Nothing could. But when he read faces in an ecstatic Nazi crowd or sized up a Polish peasant on a midnight raid for weapons, he remained attentive, vigilant, and in control, a man remarkably free of self-pity. Despite the harrowing circumstances he describes, Stevens managed to restrain his emotions, to resist the single outburst that would have cost him all, though he admits that this very coolness sometimes put him right in the lion's mouth.

To gain even a hint of the tension Stevens bore throughout the war, consider a few scenes comprising his story. Journeying at the war's outbreak from Kalisz to Warsaw, then on to Lithuania, he passes through a host of dangers: to escape the Nazis would likely put him in the hands of the Soviets; to escape the Russians costs his living amongst Lithuanian nationalists and anti-Semites. Even in his most secure harbor, the small village of Rukojnie, his refuge from the Vilnius ghetto, the German-speaking Stevens found himself immediately commissioned by the village priest to return to Vilnius and demand that the Nazis restore church property earlier confiscated by the Communists. At risk of being recognized on the streets, he nevertheless performs his charge, and with a flair even he might not previously have imagined. The scene culminates with Stevens, caught up in his part, demanding from a Nazi officer help for the church, a bold performance, he later realized, that might very well have ended with a bullet. Returning to live amongst the Polish Catholics, then, he is cited by the priest as a model for the parish, making the disguise of his Jewishness even more crucial. To compound his dilemma, Stevens is soon asked to join the resistance movement. He swears his oath on a cross and then lives with two co-workers, the Polish boys, Jan and Tolek, whose father had been a proud anti-Semite. An attractive and vigorous young man from the city, Stevens must remain aloof from the country girls by feigning physical modesty (a task in the earthy culture of the Lithuanian farm) and hiding the evidence of circumcision that would bring on disaster. Even after the Nazis were defeated, he had to decide in an instant whether to join the Russian army or to hide from them in a barn.

This partial list of the many pressures Joseph Stevens endured during the war shows how impressive was his career as a partisan. The easiest and safest way of life would have been simply working on the farm and avoiding the Resistance. For Stevens, though, being in harm's way was the Jewish reality of those years as well as a matter of self-assertion and self-respect. There are many accounts of Jews hiding from the Nazis; indeed, some of the most stirring fiction by survivors such as Ida Fink and Aharon Appelfeld has dealt with terrors that Anne Frank could never have imagined. Nor is there any shortage of memoirs recounting years in the forests among the partisans or within the various underground movements. What makes Stevens's story so valuable, I believe, is the way it unites the survivor's tale with that of the partisan's. All who resisted the Nazis knew the penalty for their actions, and Stevens, a partisan *and* a Jew, was caught in a double-bind. A simple mistake, even a wound that would be treated by his comrades or a sympathetic physician, and all would be lost. That he was not only a fighter but a group leader indicates the esteem in which Stevens was held by his wartime colleagues — finally, a community that never really knew him.

In a memorable moment from his narrative, however, Stevens recounts letting his guard down, letting the mask fall for an instant. The war was nearly over and he had returned to the family apartment in the liberated city of Kalisz — number six Piłsudzki, but changed to number six Stalin. When he knocked at the door a drunken man answered and, after hearing Stevens's request for information about his family, slammed the door in his face. Writing five decades later, Stevens says, "I can still hear the loud boom it made." He soon learned that all of his family had been deported to the Warsaw ghetto and that none had returned. Realizing that there was nothing left for him in Kalisz, a city whose 29,000 Jews by war's end numbered barely 350, he decided to leave Poland altogether. He stopped one last time at his former family home to retrieve his meager bundle and to thank the drunk's daughter for allowing him a night's rest in his own bed. Perhaps he also wanted to have a last look. Again, Stevens was confronted by the drunken father, who told him that leaving would save his life; the old man held an important job as a coal distributor and was allowed to keep a gun. Sooner or later, he said, he would shoot him. Stevens's response was quick and sure, an outburst of relief, perhaps, after years of acting: "This is an important job, being drunk at home. I am not afraid of guns; the Germans did not shoot me. It was the opposite: I was shooting them. The best thing for you would be if you would shoot yourself."

If that moment in his former home represents Stevens's break with his past life, his transition to a new one was neither easy nor expeditious. Like many Jews who had survived the horrors of the 1940s, he soon found himself at the mercy of a communist system which, though not genocidal, was just as deadly for a man from a prosperous business-owning family. Despite Stevens's early success putting a Breslau lithography company back in running order, he knew that working in Communist Poland would never be satisfying for one who took pride in his occupation. Like others, he wished to emigrate to the United States. His journey, much like his incognito life among the Poles, Lithuanians, Germans, and Russians, would not be without its ironies. To get to America, he had to escape Poland and cross into Austria, the very place from which he had first fled the Nazis in 1938. And from Vienna, he would later find himself in Stuttgart waiting for a visa and suffering his German printer-colleagues' complaints about the post-war "abuses" to which West Germany was subject.

Once set in the United States, Stevens's story, so much bound to Europe's in the first half of the century, now moves in a direction highly American. Stevens's account of his early years in this country, when viewed as a survivor memoir, may at first seem like a digression. But the very qualities which had helped him live through the war — vigilance, perception, discipline — are honored by the American dream and would ensure his success here, first in Detroit with National Lithographic Company and then in Grand Rapids with his own company. That he changed his name from Szczecinski to Stevens, a common move by earlier-century immigrants, may cause unease in today's multicultural reader. For Stevens, however, it was, like so many acts and gestures in his storied life, not a matter of politics but of efficiency and common sense. He is also wry enough to recognize that even the simplest of acts can entail unanticipated complications. He learned only after the court proceeding that "Stevens" could be spelled with either a *v* or *ph*.

Did life in America finally relax Joseph Stevens? Make him less vigilant? That a survivor, this brave and prescient man, could be forced out of his own company by wily partners may have been, as he says, due to his "business inexperience and naiveté." But one also suspects that two decades in the United States had quite naturally allowed him to drop his guard, to let the man in hiding fade into the background of his life. Stevens's willingness to bring that figure back on stage, first before classroom audiences at Grand Valley State University and now in this book, is a generous gesture, whose impact will extend far beyond the sons to whom he dedicates his narrative.

When Hitler entered Vienna in triumph, Stevens was himself a college student. Watching amidst an excited crowd gathered to hear the Nazi leader speak, a foreigner masking his Jewishness, a witness already to Jews humiliated on the streets, could he have imagined that his path across the stage of the twentieth century would again make him a performer speaking to college students and, through his writing, to future generations? Six decades later, Hitler and his world have been buried in the dark night. Joseph Stevens often greets the sun of each new day in Israel. Would even this consummate actor have dared to believe such a script?

CHAPTER ONE

✦

Saturday, March 12, 1938, is a date I will never forget. I was a foreign student in Vienna and this Saturday should have been like all the others. I was renting a room on Albertstrasse from an older Czech couple. Normally, I would have breakfast brought to my room by Mrs. Svoboda. There would be delicious Viennese rolls, butter, marmalade, coffee, and milk, with eggs and sweet rolls on occasion. Then I would take a streetcar to the front of my college on Banhoffstrasse to attend an art class, the only subject scheduled on Saturdays from nine to one. The class was held in the art gallery on the top floor of our building. Drab by today's standards, it was a corner room with a glass wall and ceiling. Chairs were arranged in a horseshoe, enabling all of us to draw the subject from a different angle. We never knew in advance what we would be drawing. It could be a geometric object, a stuffed animal, a life model (nude, on occasion), but it always had to be drawn with pencil or charcoal stick.

This particular Saturday I did not go to school. All schools and offices were closed. Radios and loudspeakers blasted out martial music and Nazi speeches. Vienna—all of Austria—was celebrating.

I did not go to school for an entire week. When students returned, the school had changed. I was greeted by large Nazi flags hanging outside, and, inside every available space was covered with Nazi slogans and more flags. Some professors and students were missing. The school was now off limits to Austrian Jews and political adversaries. Almost everyone wore a small swastika in his lapel. Those who did not were considered anti-Nazis, enemies of the nation. What a difference from the week before! Then, most Austrians displayed patriotism and allegiance to their nation by wearing Austrian tricolor emblems. I wore a small metal pin: *"Ausländer,"* or foreigner.

About sixty percent of the students in my school were from other countries. In the halls one could hear conversations in many languages, as if it were the United Nations building. There were two American students, said to have been sent by the Ford Motor Company. Some of the foreign students never returned to school; they must have gone home.

Weeks earlier, Vienna had already been in an uproar. Fights on the streets between Austrian Nazi groups and Austrian patriots were becoming more frequent. When on March 11, 1938, at Hitler's ultimatum Austrian Chancellor Kurt Schuschnigg resigned and appointed Seyss Inquart, Minister of the Interior, in his place, everyone realized that the era of Austria's independence had ended.

On March 12, 1938, I saw for the first time German troops marching in Vienna. It was not like seeing them on posters, in newspaper photos, or in black-and-white movies. They were in living color, creating fear for some, sadness and despair for others—but for most, an overwhelming, wild enthusiasm. The city was dressed up with German Nazi flags and huge banners. The streets were spread, littered, with tiny swastikas die cut from old newsprint.

Good Morning

The city looked jubilant. The most popular greeting on the street became popular overnight: "Heil Hitler!" Those who opposed Nazism were not visible. Many had been arrested or were waiting to be arrested. Others tried to stay out of the public eye as much as possible. It was too late for resistance.

The weeks preceding the Anschluss ("union" to the Germans; "annexation" to objecting Austrians) had been marked by political fights in Parliament and street fights among groups of the young. Austrian flags had been painted with swastikas and otherwise desecrated, but on this Saturday only Nazi flags were visible. Austria disappeared. Later, I saw maps showing the Greater German Reich of the future. They included Austria, Czechoslovakia, and other European countries later conquered. In the years following I realized how blind the world had been not to have been able or willing to recognize Hitler's intentions, so openly publicized in advance.

The days that followed the Anschluss, horrifying to non-Nazis, were full of glory to Nazi supporters. The Viennese Metropolitan Hotel was now Gestapo Headquarters. As a gesture to the masses, they opened the doors of the larger Jewish department stores so people could help themselves to whatever they wanted. Today we call it looting. The televised pictures of looting we see occasionally remind me of the scene in front of Vienna's largest clothing store, Krupnick. People dragged out more merchandise than they could handle. All the while they were under the protection of uniformed Austrian Nazis.

On another occasion, I saw a happy and laughing group of people clustered on the street. I went closer to see what was going on. There were several Jews, young and old, on their knees cleaning the street. One was using his hat; others, a handkerchief or a shirt; another, a tooth-brush. As I approached the group and realized what was happening, one of the young punks stepped on the hand of the old man using his hat and ordered him to clean harder and faster. The bystanders burst out laughing.

There were many other atrocities, kicking, spitting, and beatings on the streets. Prominent people were arrested, never to be heard of again. A few of my friends had also disappeared. Their families could not learn their where-abouts. I tried to help as much as I could; but other than giving moral support, running errands, mailing letters, and shopping, there wasn't much I could do.

The most dramatic of my experiences in Nazi Vienna was watching Hitler's visit on that Saturday, March 19, 1938. Curious to see him, I joined the masses of people gathered at the Heldenplatz (previously Hoffburg). Once I was on my way, no return was possible. No one was going in the opposite direction, so I had to move with the stream of people and wait until the ceremony was over. I could see Hitler from a distance, observe his wild gestures, hear his screams on the loudspeakers. The organized shouts of the people were deafening. Hitler talked about the mission of Germany. I didn't sing, salute, or shout "Heil!" I was not wearing any Austrian, German, or Nazi insignia. I was, therefore, seen as a suspicious character right away. A fellow on my side gave me a dirty look. Immediately and with a friendly smile, I pointed to my lapel. Another asked me why I did not shout "Heil." In a loud voice, so that others near me could hear, I said that I was told that as an Ausländer I was not authorized to do so. Again, I gave a friendly gesture and expression and pointed to my lapel. The people were absorbed by what was going on and didn't push me any further. I encountered the same kind of experience on numerous occasions afterward. The lapel pin seemed to work like magic, as they still respected foreigners to some extent.

Later, I realized how naive I had been and how much I had risked by wanting to go to the Heldenplatz. My blond hair and "Aryan" looks were on my side; nevertheless, it was a big gamble, a stupid undertaking, especially for a Polish Jew.

My parents soon called me on the phone and insisted that I return home. I explained to them that I was safe and that they shouldn't worry. I wanted to finish the school year. Finally, I had to say good-bye to old Vienna, the Vienna I knew before the Anschluss. I went home.

Even though I took an express train, the trip via Czechoslovakia took over twenty-four hours. As a youngster I had traveled to various countries with my parents, so I was used to the customs inspections and remembered my father always giving us instructions as to how to act: never panic or act nervous, always keep calm, declare everything that should be declared, and open your suitcases before you are asked. But this time the customs inspectors, two Austrians and one German, took the time to inspect everyone's luggage thoroughly. When they came to me, one of them, inspecting my documents, said, "Ah—a student?" He was mostly interested in the small suitcase which had books, notepads, samples of my work, and a tied-up white sack made out of a pillowcase. He took each book out, read the title, and fanned the pages to see if I was hiding any money or letters between the pages. He also went through my notepads and files of loose pages. They were mostly college essays.

He then asked me what I was hiding in the sack. I told him that it was my dirty laundry, which I had not had an opportunity to have washed before I left. I could see on his face an expression of triumph, that he had finally found something illegal or contraband. In a tone that was more an order than a request, he asked me to open it. When I untied the sack and slid the clothing partly out, he said, "Let's find out how dirty they really are." At that moment I realized that he had expected the dirty laundry to have been stuffed in the sack and not neatly folded. I had folded it to save space. This made him even more suspicious. He picked up one piece at a time, examined all of the seams, and, after he was finished, sarcastically told me that I could refold it. I did not want to show him my anger. On the other hand, I did not want to give him satisfaction, so I slowly started to stuff—not fold—my dirty laundry.

On the Czechoslovakian border, only my passport and transit visa were checked. The luggage stayed on the shelf since in Prague the car had been uncoupled and joined to a train going to Posen. At home I was greeted as if I had come from another planet. We had visitors constantly, family and friends wanting to know how Viennese life under Hitler really was. I had to tell the same story over and over to everyone who asked.

On many occasions I mentioned Hitler's speech and the "Mission of the German Empire," graphically presented on the maps of Europe which I had seen distributed in Vienna. No one took my statements seriously. Hitler couldn't fight all of Europe. If he tried, he would be defeated by strong countries like England and France. This is what everyone thought.

Good Morning

Before I returned from Vienna I had been making big plans for myself. Naturally, I knew that I would be working in the family printing plant. I felt that in Vienna I had learned all the newest techniques and processes used in the graphic arts industry. At that time, the "Graphische," as we called the Federal Graphic Institute of Learning and Research, was considered to be the best in Europe. A rival in Leipzig, Germany, had lost its glamour and prestige under the Nazi regime. I assumed that as a reproduction technician for the graphic arts industry with financial, business, and technical management training, I had better technical and managerial knowledge than anyone working in the family's plant. How shocked I was when my father announced in the plant that I would be working there and added, "and now we can start teaching Joe the profession." Later he instructed employees that I shouldn't be shown any favoritism and should be treated like anyone else starting from the bottom. And that is where I did start. I could not understand why my dad would do something like that to me.

I loved my father dearly, as I did all the members of my immediate family. We were very close and loving. My parents always provided me with anything I needed or wanted. My older brother and I were never on a fixed salary or allowance. Whenever we needed cash for personal expenses we took it from the business's cash register, recorded the amount, and initialed it. We were never questioned about our expenses. My parents treated us with overwhelming trust, as partners. They realized that we would not spend any more than necessary. I knew that eventually my older brother and I would own and manage the plant. My younger sister would be entitled to the same partnership when she grew up, if she wished. We knew the plans for the future of the plant because our parents told us. This was the custom. The children would not have to pay for the business; they were part of it. As long as the parents were alive and wanted to manage the plant, we knew that we would always obey and respect their orders or wishes.

Because I loved and respected my father I never got around to asking him why, in my opinion, he had embarrassed me in front of all those people. I did ask my mother once. She answered, "You know that your dad didn't mean to hurt you." My mother was a wonderful woman. As long as I could remember, since I had been a child, she always worked six days a week. She managed the printing plant office and the office supply business which we also owned. By today's standard, one would call her a career woman. But she was a loving and caring mother also. She could always tell if something was wrong by the looks on our faces and was always worrying about our health and welfare.

Unfortunately, I never had an opportunity later to show her my gratitude. She was murdered in Auschwitz, together with my father and sister. My brother was transported to Lublin during the liquidation of the Warsaw ghetto, and was murdered there. I was told that when my father went to their "home" in the ghetto one day, he found that my mother and sister had been taken to the railroad depot. He went to be with them. So he was also transported to their tragic destination.

My father had been very respected and well-known in the community. People used to visit him constantly at his office, asking for assistance, advice, or help. His office door was open to anyone who needed him. We, the family, considered that an intrusion and interference with his business activities. He felt differently. For him, helping others came first, before business.

Later in my adult life I finally understood why, when I had returned from Vienna, my father placed me in such an embarrassing position. Instead of being dissatisfied, I should have been grateful to him. I realize that he wanted me to work side by side with the people in the plant. By doing so, I developed close ties to them. I learned what made them satisfied and dissatisfied, their hardships, moods, and feelings. I developed knowledge of the psychology of a laborer and of a professional who works for others. This experience was a great asset when, after the war, I managed plants in Europe and later in the United States. When in 1956, I opened my own plant in Grand Rapids, I worked side by side with my employees. I worked harder and longer hours than anyone else. I never expected people to produce what I was not able to myself.

Only after coming to America, did I understand my father's private jokes. He gave nicknames to many of the employees—Hurry, Speedy, Lazy, Funny, Easy, Sleepy, Moody, Sloppy, and so on. Since he was the only person who spoke English, these were only funny-sounding names. It was not until I came to the United States and learned English that I understood the meanings of the names and their associations with their bearers.

As a young man, my father had spent several years in Denver, Colorado. He also visited the New York World's Fair in 1939. He liked the American lifestyle, and our plant was also run the American way. The name of our business was "Speed Printing Plant," translated from the German *Schnelldruckerei* (*Drukarnia Pospieszna* in Polish). Almost all of the equipment was electrically driven, although hand- and foot-powered machinery was not an uncommon sight at this time. My father tried to keep up with new developments in the graphic arts industry. Our plant was one of the first to have equipment for color relief printing. Using paper with watermarks from the paper mill was very prestigious, but it was also very expensive. My father developed an affordable way to print a fake watermark that closely resembled the genuine product. My father also introduced his own procedure to simplify the embossing and debossing processes.

Another time, he approached the owner of a large toy manufacturer, a good client, with the idea of directly printing onto children's blocks, a process much faster and more economical than painting them or pasting printed paper onto them. My brother designed a special adjustment for one of the presses that then allowed printing on wood of various thicknesses.

I once submitted a mockup carton to the same toy company for their wooden, rubber-band-powered biplane. They accepted it immediately, so later I made other photographic designs for their packaging. This started by accident. One day I was admiring the planes and decided to photograph them on a crudely designed runway with grass in the background and two more parked planes on the edge. I photographed this setup and, to my surprise, the prints looked like real planes at an airport. The toy manufacturer was so impressed that most of his new cartons were from then on designed photographically instead of hand-drawn.

Not long after I returned home from Vienna, I involved myself in a project that seemed to me then a funny experience. My dad and my brother were always figuring out some new thing or working on improvements of the old. The new project involved a patented writing pen which they named "Start." This was before ball-point pens had been heard of and when a fountain pen was a luxury. Schools and the majority of offices and homes used pens that were basically a wooden handle into which a steel nib was inserted by hand. These nibs had to be replaced when they rusted, broke from use or being dropped on the floor, became dirty with ink, or when a simple change in hardness or width was needed. A similar type of pen handle with changeable nibs can occasionally still be seen in use by calligraphers.

Back then, when a pen was left many times to dry with ink on it, it dried so hard that removing the nib could be a chore. Everyone accepted this as normal though. Young students always had ink-stained fingers because they usually did not wrap the steel nibs to protect their hands when they wiggled and struggled to remove the old ones. Anyway, my dad came up with the idea of a pen handle containing a light spring that could effortlessly eject an old steel nib by itself. The handle was sturdy with a beautiful, shiny finish. The end was also smoothly finished, which would be appreciated by people who had the habit of putting their pens in their mouths. The Start pen had an end that was rounded like a ball. But the whole idea of the pen was that, by pressing on a clean part of the handle, the old steel nib could be ejected so a new one could be inserted.

Promotional literature, very modern for its time, included a color brochure illustrating the easy use of the Start pen. When I came to the United States after the war, I was fortunate to find at my Uncle Mike's house an unused pen and a lengthy circular describing its features — in Polish. My father had mailed it to him when he took his invention to market.

Production of the pen began in the finished basement of the printing plant after stamping machinery had been specially designed. After stamping a piece from a soft steel band, the machine used additional dies to bend it into the proper shape. After being stamped "Pat" (for patent pending), the shaped pieces went to a small drum where they were polished to remove rough edges left by the press. To avoid changing their shape, the drum had fine leather scraps that acted as a polishing agent. Then to retrieve the steel pieces from the "bath," magnets were used. The polished soft springs were then dumped into heavy cylinders filled with heated oil to harden them, after which they were cleaned and inserted into wooden pen handles. Each pen was tested manually. Rejects were taken apart; too-soft springs were hardened again, but those that were too hard usually snapped. Today this process might be described as quality control.

The unfinished wooden handles were produced outside by a woodworking firm. They were milled from hard wood and were very smoothly finished. The painting was done inside. Each handle slid onto a board holding fifty pens to be painted simultaneously. The board slid upside down into a "guillotine" and was then lowered into a bath of white primer, raised, and turned upright for drying. The process was repeated for the coral red paint and again for clear lacquer that gave the color a bright, shining look. The whole mechanism looked something like a square wishing well or a rig drilling a square oil well.

One day, trouble began. Some batches of fifty pens were coming out defective and had to be relacquered, over and over. One side of the handles was dull. The paint manufacturers offered replacements and different types of lacquers. Defective pens were sent to them for examination, but no one could come up with a diagnosis. Other manufacturers' lacquers were tried, but this didn't help either. We then thought it must not be the fault of the lacquers but of something else. Lacquering was tried on a Sunday when all was quiet, in the thought that vibration from the printing presses located on the main floor above caused the problem. But that did not explain why all the batches were not defective. No one had a solution. Rooms were changed; windows were closed, even though they were the only ventilation from the heavy fumes. I don't remember everything that we tried, but I do remember everyone's frustration.

One day I decided to get completely involved in the lacquering process—not to take over the work but to observe the operation constantly and inform the lacquer manufacturer at what moment the dulling started. It puzzled me that the dulling occurred always on one side. I stayed close, inhaling the fumes and burning my eyes from watching every second. This time, to my frustration, everything went perfectly. All my effort went for nothing. Batch after batch came out with no defective pieces.

When my dad came and saw what was going on, he smilingly suggested that I should be there all the time. I knew, though, that he didn't want me even to visit the area because of the fumes. After he left, we proceeded with production and, to my shock, I noticed that the front side of one batch was starting to dull. First I thought that my father must have brought something in that was still in the air, some fumes or particles that had been on his suit.

But at the same time I had been aggravated by the happy whistling of the worker dipping the pens. As he whistled the front side of the batch had dulled! Naturally, he was blowing air. That had been the cause of the disaster all along — such a simple thing. I asked him to stop whistling and talking and to dip the same batch again. It came out perfectly and dried to a beautiful gloss. The case was solved!

I became a hero in our family with little effort on my part. Everyone was happy that the production of Start could finally proceed without problems. And I felt good that my previous feelings about whistling had been justified; I had always been annoyed when someone whistled while he worked, no matter where it was. I don't know why, but I have always had an aversion to whistling.

Always something new was brewing in the plant. My father decided to install fire-fighting equipment, hoses and extinguishers. I didn't know how to use them, so I decided to join the volunteer fire department to learn about fire fighting and prevention. I didn't learn much about prevention, but I got first-hand experience with fire fighting and drinking. The training started with exercises to see how fast I could jump into a fireman's suit plus gear and helmet. The gear was a small ax and a coil of heavy rope, both hooked to my belt. The rope, called a lifeline, had to be coiled very tightly and meticulously, without a twist. Later I learned why.

We trained on a wooden tower, which was actually a flat wooden wall four stories high, with supports behind and openings that represented windows. I was shown how to remove a hook ladder from the fire truck, run with it to the tower, hook onto the window sill of the first "floor," climb up while straddling the sill, pull the ladder behind me and hook it up to the next floor. I repeated the whole process until I found myself on the fourth floor and reversed the process to climb down to the ground. Another time I did this exercise with a fire hose attached to my belt. Still another time, upon reaching the fourth floor, I was instructed to jump to the ground.

Always attached to my belt was a small ax and a rope, both required equipment. I had to securely fasten one end of the rope to the window sill and throw the other to the ground, making sure it was looped through a heavy metal spring hook on my belt. Then I had to hold the rope below the metal loop and rappel to the ground, pushing myself away from the wall with my feet, like a mountain climber. I could control my speed by adjusting the angle of the rope relative to the loop, to keep it from burning my palms. I was afraid, when I heard the order to jump the first time, that it might be my last time. I was not sure I could land on the ground in one piece. But the exercise went better than I had expected. From that point on, all the exercises which had looked dangerous at first became almost routine.

My parents were not fond of my involvement with the fire department, especially because of what followed the exercises or a real fire. It was customary for the crew to visit a bar to "soothe" their throats from the smoke. I wished I could have ordered a glass of warm milk, which I ended up with anyway when I returned home. At the bar, though, I settled for the malt beer, which I did in fact like very much. I was the only one who drank the dark, sweet beer, but I was tolerated because I was the youngest in the group. Once in a while I had a shot of vodka (straight ninety-proof) with a snack of hot kielbasa, to the cheers of the group. To soothe their throats from the smoke, they celebrated and had a good time. I think they found a good excuse to get high.

Joseph Stevens

Our family life was proceeding normally. I was involved socially with a group of old friends and acquaintances. Politically, however, I felt increasingly uneasy, especially when tuned in to German radio. During that insecure and volatile period we tried not ever to miss the news broadcasts.

When I was very young our family got its first radio. It was a crystal set, and I was very impressed with it. I proudly demonstrated it to other kids, showing them how to manipulate the connecting handle, the only tuner the radio had. Because everyone wanted to wear the earphones, they had to share them by turning one ear piece outwards. Later my family also had a second radio that we called the "big" one. It had exposed silver tubes and was powered by a separate, heavy wet cell battery placed on a shelf. The next one had nine tubes, but the whole apparatus was enclosed. At that time the quality and performance of a radio was measured by the number of tubes. The more it had, the greater its reception and the better the radio. We also lengthened our outdoor antenna. Our last radio was a huge Telefunken Superheterodyne. When its volume was turned up, it could be heard in every room. This was state-of-the-art equipment. Television was only science fiction. I was fascinated by the book *Orkish' Televisor*, one of my favorites. My dream was to own the featured magic box and focus it on any place in the world to receive transmitted pictures. I didn't realize then that I would live in times when similar equipment would be available to anyone—and in living color! But the radio was the medium from which we received international news fastest.

When something went wrong with the equipment, my brother was the one who knew how to adjust and repair it. He was always very technically inclined. My family loved telling a story about the rocking horse he had as a young boy. (I later inherited it when he got a new wooden wagon powered by long pedals and steered by a set of wide fancy handlebars). My brother was always enhancing the looks of the horse by sticking fancy thumbtacks in it and decorating it with colored strings and ribbons with large buttons, The latter were supposed to represent medals. He once removed the winding stem from my mother's expensive gold watch and nailed it to the horse's head, to make it look like a general's horse. While this was supposed to have gotten him into quite a bit of trouble, I had the feeling that my parents were actually very proud of his inspiration. Knowing my parents, I am sure that they didn't punish him very severely for his mischief.

The only creature in the house that did not like the radio was our dog. When the news came on he always ran for quiet. He was a black Newfoundland, husky and very strong, named Owens — after the American Olympic athlete, Jesse Owens. When I walked the dog on a leash, the exercise was for me because I had to hold him back. He was stronger than I and always wanted to walk faster than I did. In the summer he was always hot in his heavy fur and loved to swim in the river. When we took him out in a rowboat, he would jump out and swim next to us (Newfoundlands are known for being very good swimmers and rescue dogs). His paws were webbed, like a duck's. Owens was a very good and obedient dog, but once in a while he got into mischief. Unfortunately, upon the insistence of our maid, we had to give him away. The maid had set the dining room table for dinner, as we were expecting company. At each setting was a plate of lettuce sprinkled with lemon juice and powdered sugar. She caught the dog in the act as he climbed onto each chair and licked the sugar from the lettuce. That did it.

But our biggest concern was the tense political situation in Europe. In October, 1938, we were shocked by the announcement of the government that all Polish Jews who had lived outside the country for more than five years would have their passports revoked. They would lose their citizenship, becoming stateless. The Germans immediately reacted by rounding up all Jews of Polish descent living in Germany, even those who had lived and worked there for thirty years. They had to leave their property behind, and were allowed to take only one suitcase or bundle. Overnight, they were taken to train stations and deported to the Polish border. German soldiers forced them at gunpoint to walk across the border, where they were left in open fields. The largest concentration of deportees was near the city of Zbąszyń, but our city, Kalisz, was fairly close to the border. When news of what was happening reached us, the Jewish community immediately organized an emergency relief operation. At first, the Polish government refused to let the refugees into the country. Seeing them was a heartbreaking experience. There were masses of people, living in the fields, exposed to rain and cold nights, lacking tents or any other shelter. But food was the highest priority. I was appointed youth group coordinator and I was told to visit a sausage manufacturer and observe the packing of long dry salamis into new wooden crates. The salamis were to be immediately transported to the border, along with cases of bread. (This was my first visit to such a place. I had never seen sausage manufacturing or so many salamis). Eventually, these unfortunate people were allowed into the country to live with other families.

We were shocked when detailed news about the

Good Morning

We were shocked when detailed news about the *Kristallnacht* of November 9th and 10th reached us. This was more ominous than what I had experienced in Vienna during the Anschluss, even worse than one of the pogroms our people have known throughout our history. It was an unbelievable disaster. We couldn't believe that a "cultured" Western country could organize such bloodshed and destruction, murdering their own citizens and patriots only because they were Jews. The Kristallnacht was organized by Nazis not only in Germany, but also in annexed Austria and the Sudetenland. In those two days hundreds of Jews were murdered, many more beaten and raped, thirteen hundred synagogues burned or vandalized, and over ten thousand Jewish homes, businesses, and other facilities confiscated or wrecked. Of the more than twenty-five thousand Jews arrested, many subsequently perished in prisons and concentration camps.

Detailed news describing German atrocities and murder kept reaching us. We organized meetings and protests and boycotted German products. Unfortunately, nothing influenced the "clean race" on its way to destroying the Jews. At that time we didn't know that this was just a beginning. We had expected that the world would undertake some action to stop Nazi crimes. But only a month before, Germany had marched into the Sudetenland, a part of then-democratic Czechoslovakia. And the world took no action.

Before the German army took over the Sudetenland, many Jews had opportunity to escape to the eastern part of Czechoslovakia. Those who did not were arrested by Nazis and shipped to concentration camps. Again Jewish property was confiscated, synagogues were looted and destroyed. The Nazis had their victory. New concentration camps were established; existing ones were enlarged and "improved" in their capacity to torture and destroy.

Years before, as a young boy, I used to go on vacation with my father in Czechoslovakia, to the world-famous spas in Karlsbad, Marienbad, and Joachimstal. One trip home in 1928, when I was ten, was especially memorable. We flew from Prague in a biplane. Naturally, my mother didn't know and would never have approved. The plane held four, including the pilot. The wind blew through the canopy, and the ride was very bumpy, a fascinating and scary experience for me. I felt like a hero when I later described the flight to the other kids. None of them had ever flown in a plane. Not many people had. Trains were used for transportation.

CHAPTER TWO
୬୬

The months before September 1, 1939, were very tense. No one really believed a war between Poland and Germany would start, but everyone was making preparations for it anyway. The older folks remembered the Great War, from 1914 to 1918, and its consequences. Newspapers were full of reports, under big headlines, about international political negotiations. The pact between France, England, and Poland made everyone feel sure that Hitler would not dare to continue the expansion of his dream of a Greater German Reich. England felt secure on its island. France's impenetrable Maginot Line was supposed to serve as a strong deterrent to Hitler's army. Poland was made to believe that its large units of supposedly well-trained, tough infantry and horse cavalry would annihilate the German army. In addition, Bem's fortifications on the river Bug were supposed to serve as a second line of defense. We were told that there was no way the German tanks could cross the river. What a farce!

At that time, I really believed in the might of the Allied forces. Sometimes, observing a Polish motorized unit passing the town, I thought it was the tops. Now I realize that the light motorized units were like toys compared to the might of the German army, which knew it could easily defeat the Polish "paper tiger."

Large gatherings were organized in town. People marched along with big bands to the outskirts of the city. Everything was done with great fanfare to appeal to the patriotism of the masses. Naively, we believed that we could dig with shovels trenches that would keep the German tanks from reaching Kalisz. Our printing plant produced large, colorful signs that appealed to the patriotism of citizens participating in the digging. All were advised to buy shovels if they did not already own them. When I think of it now, the picture of people marching with shovels held like rifles looks silly. Motorized digging equipment was unheard of at that time.

Appeals for money for the Red Cross and hospitals were made on a large scale. Black paper and tape for blacking out windows against possible night air attacks was in demand and eventually in short supply. During the nights, all the streetlights were kept off and special patrols issued tickets with fines to whoever had light leaking from their windows. Naturally, the purpose of all this was to hide the city from German planes. But bombarding the city during the day could be easily accomplished. No air defense existed, except for a few machine guns and rifles. (Many platoons in the Polish infantry were equipped with a then-secret long rifle, operated by a specially trained sharpshooter.) Even during the night, the Germans could drop small parachutes holding magnesium flares, as they had at other locations. A siren installed on top of the fire station was supposed to warn people of incoming planes, so there would be enough time for them to go into the basements of their houses. There were a few public shelters, mainly against poison gas, equipped with hand-operated ventilators in case power was knocked out.

At home, the big Telefunken Superheterodyne radio

was blasting all the time. It was tuned mainly to the station from Breslau-Gleiwitz, most of whose programs were not local but from the German national network. It ran propaganda, martial music, political speeches, and, very often, Hitler's speeches—which reminded me of my days in Vienna. The station we listened to next most often was Radio Warsaw. Its tone was similar: not conciliatory, but self-assured that we were strong and mighty. (Later, the same station informed the populace about strategic withdrawals from the front and "victories," at the same time it called on regrouping for the defense of Warsaw. They appealed to the patriotism of citizens in a time when all was chaos and in shambles.) All the stores were busy. Everyone was purchasing whatever he or she could. People were confused and very nervous. No one really knew what to do. Some decided to leave the town temporarily and move east. They felt uncomfortable being so close to the German border. Students didn't know if the schools would reopen on time after the summer break. Opening day was always September 1.

"Tax collectors," of whom I had not been previously aware, visited businesses in order to collect taxes, especially those businesses owned by Jews. To my surprise, a few days before the outbreak of the war such a "Polish patriot" stopped at our family office requesting money for income taxes we supposedly owed. When my mother gave him some paper money, he asked her whether she was hoarding change. I imagine he thought that the metal coins were worth more than the paper zlotys. I am sure that he never transferred any money to his office. Everything operated in great confusion.

Another incident at that time shocked me. I was helping in the family store, among other chores, selling office supplies and paper products. We were very busy, as were all the other stores. I was dressed in my fireman's uniform. Because of the political situation, we were all on alert status. At the sound of the city sirens signaling oncoming German planes, we would be ready to jump into our fire fighting gear and into action. We heard the sirens on many occasions, but each time were told "they went to bombard other places." While I was in the store among our other customers, a Polish army officer walked in. He was dressed in a spotless, well-fitted uniform with the shiny boots that were the mark of all Polish officers. (They were usually polished by a low-ranking soldier assigned to the officer as a personal adjutant—essentially, a valet.) The appearance of the uniform was one of the most prestigious parts of being an officer; it was supposed to make an impression. From the sidelines, the quality of the weapons seemed to be of less importance. Cavalrymen usually wore long swords at their sides attached to perfectly polished belts.

The particular officer who entered our store looked at me haughtily and asked what a Jew was doing in a fireman's uniform. His question stunned me because it was intentionally anti-Semitic. Although war with the Germans was imminent, on the subject of Jews many agreed with Hitler's theories. It became fashionable for many Poles, especially army officers, to make openly anti-Semitic remarks.

A few years before, at the age of eighteen, I had been called to take the physical examination for compulsory service in the Polish army. I passed without restrictions and was assigned to the officers' school. I received an official deferment because of my studies in Vienna, without which I would not have been allowed to leave the country. Of course, even without the postponement, I wouldn't have been accepted into the military academy. Very seldom did a candidate with the notation of "Mosaic persuasion" have a chance to become a Polish officer. I would be put off for a year, and year after year after that, always for the same official reason: "Overcrowding at the academy" (named Podchorążówka). Most men in good physical condition with a high school education were considered officer material. Credit was also given for students who had graduated from the equivalent of ROTC, the official high school preparation for army training. At the fire department, although I was a novice and by their standards a delicate weakling, my military status gained me respect. (I also took driving lessons and my motorcycle driving test on the fire department grounds. I remember being taught by a fat fireman on an old, small fire truck with a Chevrolet engine.)

When a military mobilization was declared, most people believed that war was imminent. I received by mail an order to report immediately to the Observation Balloons Battalion at the military base at Okęcie near the Warsaw airport. That raised the question of how to get there. The trains were overcrowded and almost unavailable. Inter-city busses were appropriated by the military, as were most private automobiles. People were purchasing horses and buggies from farmers for enormous sums. They could use them as transportation to evacuate. Many carried large suitcases with their belongings. They were fleeing east, as far as they could get from the German border. They expected any war to be very short. It was short, but the results were very different from what everyone expected. Radio Warsaw played Chopin to calm the populace as the Germans from the west and the Soviets from the east overran Poland in only seventeen days. This was the Blitzkrieg, the beginning of World War II.

Fortunately for me, I learned that one of the fire engines and some personnel were being evacuated to Łódź, about half the distance to Warsaw. I was surprised to see among us people like our chief, who also happened to be the main editor of the city's largest daily newspaper, *Gazeta Kaliska,* and a few other big shots, "patriots" who were running from the Germans. On August 31, 1939, at noon, we took off. I loaded my backpack with some immediate personal necessities and a change of underwear, and I took my bicycle with me. I did not realize then that that was the best thing I could have done.

Before leaving home I had had the urge to take my motorcycle instead. It was a light Austrian-made 250cc "Puch," with which my brother and I had had lots of fun. I also had a small mishap once. One weekend, I was riding with my good school friend, Arthur Braun, on the back, proceeding towards a cottage in Krzyżówki. From a hill I had spotted on a side road a young cowherd leading cows to pasture. They took up half the road, so I planned to pass them on the left. But the closer I came, the more of the road they took up. I squeezed left, hoping that I would have enough room to pass, but at the last moment one cow decided to move, blocking me completely. Instead of running into the cow I steered the bike into a shallow soft ditch on the side of the road. I had slowed enough that not much damage was done. The right foot pedal was slightly bent (we were able to fix it using a stone as a hammer), and my right pant leg was torn (the split seam served well as a vent). When I met him after the war my friend and I joked about the accident. He survived the Holocaust in Nancy, France, where he had been studying medicine.

Good Morning

Before I left, I said good-bye to my family, which was very hard for me. I felt as if I were deserting them. I did not realize that that would be the last time I would see them. I still remember my father's parting words: "Be well. Do the things you are supposed to do and don't go out of your way to become a hero." He meant a dead hero, but he didn't say that. He said that because he knew me well and did not want me to show off, as he had heard from friends I sometimes did in the fire department. The whole family worried about my going to the military with war imminent. None of us realized that the rest of the family was in the greater jeopardy. I feared I might not see them again because I, not they, might not survive the war. No one then would have guessed otherwise, that the immediate future would be so barbaric.

I arrived at noon at the fire department and we took off. Halfway through the trip we felt hungry and decided to stop at a farmhouse to buy some food. The farmers refused to sell because thousands of people coming before us had tried to do the same. Zlotys, the Polish currency, had become almost worthless. They wanted gold or other valuables. No one had those, or at least they said they didn't. I had a gold watch that I was wearing on my arm, but I wouldn't have considered at the time exchanging it for food. (I received the watch from an uncle, who had visited us from his home in Denver quite a few years earlier.) The group stopped at a side road by some poor farm and decided to take things into their own hands. A city boy who had never been closely exposed to farm life, I would never forget that scene.

Although farmers hid everything from the masses of city refugees, the group learned where the unfortunate farmer kept his chickens. They grabbed a few, chopped off their heads with a fireman's ax and let the blood run onto the grass. They plucked the feathers, chopped off the wings and feet, cleaned the insides, and cut them into pieces. They collected some branches and made a fire; got some big, heavy, black pots and some salt from the frightened farmer; collected vegetables and potatoes from the field; and cooked them. This was a first lesson in survival for a city boy who had never laid a hand on a cooking pot. Our housekeeper wouldn't let me.

At first I felt like gagging; but when I got my portion of chicken soup with lots of potatoes and some chicken parts, it tasted mighty good. I tried to overlook the lack of hygiene and the way the meal was provided. We collected some money for the farmer, but still left him very unhappy.

Satisfied and not hungry anymore, we took off and again reached the highway, crowded with people. Most everyone was dragging something. Some were pushing small handwagons holding bundles and suitcases. A very few had horse-drawn wagons, piled with people or belongings. An occasional bicyclist went by. Both sides of the road moved in only one direction—east. Because of the crowds and slow pace we couldn't pick up any speed. Once in a while when an army vehicle passed, people were forced to squeeze to the right and give way, giving us a chance to follow. The vehicle usually turned onto a side road, leaving us in the same situation as before. We were tempted to use our siren or bell; but with everyone's temper on edge, we did not dare take advantage of them. We were occasionally able to edge slowly past the people and traffic in front of us.

When we reached Łódź I said good-bye to my comrades. They wished me luck when I took my bike and backpack and went off. I had the urge to look up my family in the town. (My father had been born in Łódź when it was the German city of Litzmannstadt, and I had much family there.) But the city was in chaos and I didn't want to lose the time. I proceeded on my bike towards Warsaw. I faced the same scene on the road and still had one hundred and fifty kilometers to go. I was lucky that the nights were bright because no one had any lights. At night I took short naps by the sides of the road, my legs always over the bike so no one would steal it, my backpack under my head. Once I must have slept very deeply, because early in the morning I woke up without my pack. I got very upset, but was happy that at least I still had my bike. Occasionally at night, I would grab hold of a horse-drawn wagon and would not have to pedal. This usually worked only until they spotted me. Once I caught myself falling asleep on my bike, almost being run under the wheels and into the spokes of a wagon. After that I was more careful. Every so often I spotted an old, broken down automobile being pulled by a horse. Either the auto was disabled or was without gasoline, which was not available for private use. It was good thing I had my bicycle instead of the motorcycle.

Finally I reached Warsaw and did not believe what I saw. The town looked almost deserted, already bombarded, with everything in disarray. When I spotted an MP foot patrol and asked for directions to my unit I was told it had been evacuated to the east to defend the border from the invading "Bolsheviks." After the pact between Hitler and Stalin, Poland was invaded from both sides.

I was tired, full of dust, and decided to stop at a friend's house to freshen up. After obtaining directions, and with much difficulty, I reached it. To my disappointment nobody was home. I found out after the war that they too, along with thousands of others, had evacuated east. I also had with me the address of a distant cousin named Ajke. I tried to reach him and, luckily, he was home. It was already evening. The first thing I had to do was to wash myself. I had never in my life seen such dirty water running off my body. I could have washed on the road at some water holes, but the thousands of people who had gone before me had made the water dirtier than I was. The drinking water situation was no better, even if you were lucky enough to get some. Almost all of it was in wells belonging to small farmers. They looked like wishing wells, with heavy wooden buckets lowered by hand on a chain or rope. Because of their heavy use, many were already dry. If you were able to get any water by dragging the bucket along the bottom of the well it was muddy and brown. A horse would not have touched it, but to us humans it meant more than gold. By then, it was late in the evening, and I went to sleep on a couch. It felt as comfortable as a bed after my naps on the dirt by the road or, at best, grass that had been trampled by thousands of people.

At the beginning of the war, the Germans bombarded Warsaw mostly by night. When incoming planes were seen the sirens blasted, warning everyone to go to a bomb shelter or basement, no matter on which floor one lived. Although it was against the rules not go to a shelter, I was so exhausted that I stayed put, not caring what would happen. (My cousin's son, Marek Ajke, reminded me of this when we met in 1994. Of his entire family, only he and his father survived. They had managed to live through imprisonment in *seven* concentration camps and finally emigrated to Bolivia.) During the night the sirens sounded several times, but many were false alarms when the planes supposedly headed in another direction. I heard some explosions, both distant and nearby, as the bombs hit the city.

Early in the morning I got some food and wanted to leave that hell as soon as possible. I did not realize that this was heaven in comparison to what I would see later. I had no idea what was in store for me and millions of other people, including my family.

I had left the city in the nick of time. A few days later the city was completely surrounded by the Germans. The electricity was cut off, along with the water, food, and all other provisions. Most of the city was destroyed by uninterrupted bombardment. The resulting fires could not be extinguished because of the lack of water. The Warsaw resistance lasted almost four weeks, finally ending when the mayor, Colonel Starzynski, surrendered the city. Hitler, himself, came to Warsaw on September 27, 1939, to review the parade of his victorious troops.

When I left, I did not know my destination, only that I would have to travel east toward the river Bug. The moment I got on my bike and started pedaling, a big black cat jumped in front of the bike. He turned his head in my direction for a moment so that I could see his big, shiny eyes. According to superstition this was a bad omen. The vision haunted me all through the war, even though I wasn't superstitious.

My experience on the road became very chaotic and dangerous, even more than before. German planes, with no opposition, approached more often, looking for military units or heading toward designated targets. When we heard the approaching planes everyone ran for cover, heading toward whatever trees or bushes were nearby. If there were none, we would spread out on both sides of the road and lie down, trying to squirm and shrink our bodies to the minimum dimension. We never knew what the planes intended to do. Sometimes they dived very low to harass people, often using machine guns or dropping bombs to destroy the road and whatever was on it. During one of the bombing runs I was lying on the ground with my face buried in the sand with my bike next to me. My mind must have frozen, and I tried to avoid hearing what was going on around me: the roar of the diving plane and the explosion of bombs. As the sound of the plane flying away dwindled and the short bursts of its machine guns ceased, I came to my senses and lifted my head. I awakened to shrieks and cries for help. A few feet in front of me I saw a body split in half, like a filleted fish. I remember the bloody insides and the ribs; the first time in my life I had seen a dead, mutilated body. I became nauseated and could not move for a while. I wondered if I was hurt, dreaming, or simply frozen. A moment later I realized what had happened. The tumult and noise were like a scene from hell. Medical help was almost nonexistent. Except for being covered with dust and dirt, though, nothing had happened to me or to the bike, my most important possession.

To tell the truth, I wondered at how lucky I was, being able to proceed without a scratch, only a little shaken up. Luck was with me in the next few years. In direct skirmishes with German units I was slightly wounded only twice. Once, had I held my right hand one inch further to the left, the bullet that scratched my wrist would have hit it, costing me my right hand (possibly my life from medical complications — the hospitals were off limits to us). Another time a piece of a hand grenade pierced my clothes and scratched my chest over my heart. Had I moved forward I wouldn't have survived. The scars remain.

Good Morning

My destination was east. During the nights, the red sky pointed to distant fires. One night the whole horizon was red. I learned that the city of Lublin was burning after a bombardment. Lublin was supposed to have had a permanent military installation and homes for several regiments. As I passed through the city in the daylight I could see the devastation. Unfortunately, the weather had been exceptionally nice. It had not rained since I had left home, and I understood it hadn't in the entire country. German planes could fly their missions day and night without a cloud to hinder them.

I noticed a line of people on one of the roads. When I approached and asked why they were standing there, I was told that they were waiting to buy bread from a bakery. Right after I got into the line, a long way down it stopped moving. The bakery had run out of bread. But they were baking another batch and were supposedly going to continue until they ran out of flour, so I continued to wait along with everyone else. One consolation was that the line behind me continued to grow longer. This was my first experience of waiting in a line to purchase food, other than while on maneuvers in the ROTC. It was another three or four hours until the line started moving again. I hoped that they would still have bread when I reached the front. People were edgy, tired and thirsty from the waiting and all else that was going on. I stayed seated on my bike the whole time, afraid to lose my place in line. When I got my loaf of bread I didn't know what to do with it. I could not hold it in my hands because it was so hot. I wrapped it in my fireman uniform jacket and tied it to my bike with the sleeves. It was a valuable possession; I had to guard it in order not to lose it. The next problem was getting some water.

On September 17, 1939, I found myself in the city of Łuck. It had already been occupied by the Russians that day. I thought that this was the end of the road for me. With no way back, I thought the war was over. I had no idea that the war would be with me for six more years, costing me my entire family and changing my life completely.

A few people tried to return west to their homes. Naively, many believed the rumors that England and France were ready to liberate the country by invading Germany from the West. My biggest worry was my family. I knew that they were under Nazi occupation and that I could not help them at all. No contact by telephone or mail was possible. I found myself alone and without resources.

Łuck was a strange city to me. I knew it only by name. Like most of the small cities in the east of Europe, it looked very primitive; but I also knew that there were many flour mills there and that some were customers of our printing business. In my family's plant we printed special oval labels for the flour sacks and supplied lead seals and hand-held brass embossers for attaching them. The one-inch-diameter seals were embossed with the name and number of the mill. My dad and brother designed the embossers to clamp the seals to the top of the flour sacks so they could not be removed without destroying them. Parts for the embossers were produced by a brass foundry and were cleaned and assembled by a machine shop. The blank seals were made in the same place as the inserts for the Start pens. As they were not steel, they did not have to be hardened, only punched out from a roll of thin metal. An engraver hand-produced the master plates with names for each embosser. I was told that all our label customers and others had also been ordering the embossers and seals.

They provided good repeat business.

When I arrived in Łuck the city was in an uproar. Russian soldiers considered it heaven — they grabbed, stole, or bought cheaply whatever was available in the privately owned stores (which most of them were). The ruble was in demand because it was now the only currency supposed to have any value. When the store owners kept their stores closed, an order was issued that they had to reopen. In no time they were emptied. Nothing was available.

My first task was to find a place to wash up and lay down my head. I was given directions to a place which looked like an old boarding house but which called itself a hotel. Fortunately, a room was available. Although no service, or anything else, was supplied, I was told that I could use an old bathtub. It took considerable persuading to buy a small piece of yellow laundry soap, a rag called a towel, and a half loaf of dark bread. As soon as I "checked in" I went to the bathtub and filled it with water. Of course, only cold water was available. I was hot, so the water I immersed in felt like ice. Shivering, I was still pleased that for the first time since leaving home I had clean water. It did not look so clean after I had washed in it, and neither did the tub. I rinsed and refilled it so I could rinse myself. The towel was so small that I left that "bathroom" half wet and lay naked on my bed to dry. Anyway, I did not have pajamas or a nightshirt. Later, I washed my shirt and the only underwear I had, hoping they would dry by morning. I didn't worry about the shirt because it was not very absorbent and dried very fast. It was a short sleeve shirt that I had bought in Vienna. I liked the blue color and the fine net pattern.

I remembered the names of only two flour mills that

were our customers. I was sure that they owed us some money because their orders for labels for various types of flour had come in constantly. As I remembered, they were not so quick to pay and their credit was usually extended for longer periods. The first mill was the largest in the area, but I was greatly disappointed when I visited. The owner wasn't there, and the mill had already been nationalized. It was administered by a self-appointed group of workers who called themselves the "Communist Workers Committee." They all acted like big shots and were proud to have set the mill free from the capitalist bourgeoisie, the rich classes. When I asked for the director, who was usually a party member or a newly made Communist, they looked at me suspiciously. I was still wearing my "dressy" fireman's uniform. The gold buttons and the epaulets made it resemble a military officer's uniform, though it was only navy blue. All officers were suspect, belonging in jail and not walking free. Officers were considered enemies of communism and the working class. The Russian soldiers on the street looked at me especially suspiciously. Later I was told that I had been lucky not to have been arrested and have my bicycle confiscated. I was also told that I had been lucky that the director of the mill did not have me arrested when he lectured me that from now on I would have to work to get some money. As a son of a bourgeois and a capitalist, I was considered an enemy of the Communists.

I tried the second mill with more luck. The owner sympathized with me and gave me some money. He said that it was not all that he owed but that he expected the mill to be nationalized at any time and he himself kicked out. He wasn't allowed to pay out anything without the approval of the "workers' board." The workers already had more to say about the running of the mill than he did. As he always had been good to the employees, they still tolerated him in the office. But he was sure he would not last long. He gave me the name and address of an old widow who might rent me a room on his recommendation.

I immediately went to her house, but she would not let me in until I told her who had referred me and how I knew him. She agreed to sublet a room and offer whatever food she could scrape up at an affordable price, but I didn't have Russian rules. Although the small basement room looked like a dungeon, I was happy to have found it and moved in immediately, with no possessions except my bike. Later, I sold it at an enormous price, one I would not have imagined before. The old widow knew people who had owned small shops from which I could buy at black market prices some immediate necessities — not from their shops, but from their homes. Most business was conducted by barter without knowledge of the Russians. This was dangerous. They could be arrested, with their possessions confiscated, and their entire families sent to Siberia.

The first thing my new landlady did was cut the shoulder straps and gold buttons from the jacket of my fireman's uniform. Everyone warned me that the Russians might mistake me for a former official, some big shot. This was the first time that the Communist soldiers had had the opportunity to see the life of people outside their own backward country. They had been indoctrinated that nowhere else in the world was life better than in Russia, that the purpose of the war was to liberate poor workers from oppression in the countries which they occupied. They were shocked by what they found, though they couldn't admit it. They were afraid to admit anything and said only what they had been taught. Cameras were nonexistent since Russians had been told only spies used them. Even if I could have gotten one, film was not available and I was told that film could only be obtained for official use, by special permission.

Russians took literally anything that was available to be purchased, stolen, or confiscated and shipped it home, without concern. It is impossible now for a Westerner to understand the culture and behavior of the Communist Russian hordes in 1939. Their army uniforms looked like rags, and their boots were torn. Later in the winter many wore torn felt boots. It was not unusual to see a soldier wearing his rifle with a rope instead of a leather strap. Sometimes, the strap was made of short pieces of rope knotted together. For even cheap watches in the worst condition, they would pay any price. They were very prestigious, coveted like a trophy. When their portraits were taken by professional photographers in town, they always posed left hand in front, coat sleeve pulled back, so everyone at home could see the wristwatch. Of course, all the local people made fun of them behind their backs.

Whenever they were asked if something was available in Russia, they gave the same answer: "We have plenty." But we knew that, for the average Russian, everything was in short supply or nonexistent. Because of bad transportation and planning, distribution across such a vast country was very poor. A product produced in one part of the country was likely unavailable in another. If it did show up in a state store, it was immediately grabbed. People stood in line and were sometimes fortunate enough to get into a store, but they didn't get to purchase what they wanted, only what was in stock and available. Standing in line, even for bread, was an accepted way of life.

Good Morning

Only Communist party members, the privileged class, had special stores, off limits to normal citizens. We thought of the soldiers as barbarous, wild people. This joke was popular at the time, and I believe it was a true story. Someone asked a soldier if they had tangerines in Russia. He answered proudly that they had plenty of tangerine factories.

The Russians started to arrest people on a large scale. They took people who had owned any business, assuming that they were anti-Communist capitalists and, therefore, their enemies. People who were suspected of being anti-Communist were often arrested for no reason and without any proof. Leaders and members of non-communist organizations were arrested, even many socialists. People who had had ties to the police, government, city administration, army, or other organizations were enemies. They tried to change their identities or hide, for people wanting to get even with someone simply pointed him out to the Russians, who had him arrested by the NKVD (secret police) and shipped to Siberia or some other isolated, frozen area in eastern Russia.

Newcomers to the city, mostly refugees from the West (I was one), were also suspicious. In the eyes of the Russians we were parasites who did not work. Many were arrested *en masse* and shipped to Russia. Everyone lived in fear, not knowing what his or her fate would be.

One morning I was walking on the street when somebody called me by name. My first reaction was fright because we always felt as if we were being hunted, and I did not recognize this person. He introduced himself as Leon Roth, an acquaintance of my brother and about his age. Leon's family in Kalisz had a business manufacturing mirrors and polished plate glass; they supplied sheet glass for the building industry. I remembered the firm name from their sign on Kanonicka Street just across from the church of Saint Kanoników. As a little boy I had often visited the church with my nanny. During a short conversation, Leon explained that he was working and had documents issued by some high Red Army officers stating that he could not be touched by any authorities. Such secure documents were exceptional.

Many families of Soviet officers had moved into confiscated or abandoned apartments. There were also new family apartment blocks near the garrison of the Polish Army, now occupied by Russian families. The Russians, who arrived in large numbers, found these apartments the epitome of luxury. They had seen nothing like them in Russia. Foreign travel was impossible to ordinary Soviet citizens—the borders were sealed, and anyone attempting to cross was shot—the only people who traveled outside the country were a small number of trusted party members on government missions. Even they went only to the relatively few countries that had relations with Russia.

During the earlier bombardments many glass windows had been shattered in the city, including those in the apartments now occupied by Russians. Men like Leon were useful to them. I don't know how he had made contact with them because he didn't know any Russian. Some improvised sign language came in handy. He needed a helper and asked me to join him. I thought that he was joking, just being nice. But he said that he could teach me the trade in no time. Never in my young life did I accept an offer so happily. All this happened in the street in a few minutes. He introduced me to an officer, telling him that he had known me for a long time from our work together, that I was a very good glass installer and glazier, and that I had always been very poor, just as he had been. Without hesitation he gave me the job. Communications with the Russians were difficult at first, but I learned faster than I had ever learned a language. I learned always to answer *"w poriadku"* — "everything is in order" — or *"harasho,"* which means "okay."

Occasionally they assigned Leon an old, small army truck and a driver, so we could transport cases of glass. I never knew that glass could be so heavy and so sharp. Until I learned to handle the sheets properly, I had plenty of cuts and bruises. And I wasn't at home with my family, had no one to baby me or worry that I might get an infection.

Leon said that I was a pretty good apprentice who did not break much glass cutting it. He seemed as concerned about wasting glass as I imagine he was in his own plant. The Russians would have accused us of sabotage if they caught us breaking it, although they themselves were very careless and rough transporting it. Sometimes a whole case was wasted. We didn't have good cutting tools, but with Leon's help I mastered the trade and its tricks surprisingly fast. We didn't have to worry about shortages of sheet glass, which was unavailable in the city. The Russians had confiscated all that was available, claiming that they had nationalized it for the benefit of poor people. Leon, having access to the warehouses where glass was stored, undertook some "private" jobs. People needed his services almost as much as those of a medical doctor, and he acted like one. Occasionally we came across a mirror in the warehouse. When we installed any piece of mirror on a wall, the residents didn't know how to thank us. It really meant something to them.

I moved in with Leon, sharing a room. The owner of the apartment, also an older widow, prepared all our meals. Not much was available on the open market because virtually everything had been confiscated by the Russians. As a premium, we had been receiving one loaf of army black bread from them. It tasted pretty good, though I couldn't have imagined eating such bread at home. We had a nice setup. At first we had nice weather, though fall started to creep in; so I obtained some clothing and flannel underwear, which came in handy later during cold weather.

We had a very demanding job but, most importantly, we had all the glass we needed and transportation. Still, we always worked under pressure. We could not choose work sites which were near each other; the most important people in the Communist hierarchy had priority. We worked in the apartments newly occupied by Russians, and couldn't believe what we saw. The apartments may have started in decent condition, but they weren't anymore. There was usually more than one family per apartment. At the time, in the better apartments, bidets were fashionable. The Russians had never seen them before and didn't know how to use them. They complained about how low the "washbasins" were. They washed their faces and their clothing in them. Sometimes, they used the toilets for the same purposes. I would not have believed it if I hadn't seen it with my own eyes. When we enlightened them, they were sure we were kidding and making fun of them. In the garrison quarters, central warm water was occasionally available. That, and one toilet per apartment, was the peak of capitalistic luxury.

I lived and worked hoping that eventually something would change for the better politically. We had no direct contact with the rest of the world by telephone, letter, or any other legal means. But, tragic news started trickling in from the west, news about atrocities against Jews, who were being executed by the Nazis in all the countries under German occupation. We almost could not believe the stories that the "lucky" ones were telling us. These people had escaped illegally and dangerously through the new German-Russian borders. Many who also tried had been caught and executed by the Germans. (After the war I learned that one of my school friends, Ed Boraks, had been caught by the Germans while crossing the border at the Bug River. He had not been trying to escape himself. In fact, he had crossed the border many times, guiding others out of German-occupied territories. He was a hero in the ghetto whose people he was helping. I later saw his picture displayed in the Yad Vashem Holocaust Museum. For his heroism he was posthumously awarded the "Virtutte Military" medal.) Even those who escaped the Germans were not safe. Many were caught at the border by Russians and were conveniently labeled spies or anti-Communists. They were often sent to Siberia or other remote, cold, uncivilized places from which they were unlikely to return.

The few who did return after the war told us about the unbelievable conditions they endured. Their worst enemies were the extreme cold and hunger. Diseases and lack of warm clothing and medical help added to their pain. One of my teenaged friends, Sophie Gill, had always been a large girl. She dropped from 175 pounds to an 80-pound living skeleton. Her mother died from hunger.

I realize now that I was lucky to have been living under the conditions I was, though I considered them intolerable at the time.

W e had unexpected news that the Russians were with-drawing from three Baltic countries: Lithuania, Latvia, and Estonia. Because we read it again and again in the official Communist newspapers, we began to believe it. They wrote that after "liberating" the working classes from bourgeois parasites, the Russians could withdraw, leaving those countries under their own governments. We knew that they would leave many of their own spies and cadres behind to monitor events. (My own experience in Lithuania later revealed that anti-Communists, national chauvinists, so-called patriots, anti-Semites, and many with ultra-right-wing views soon emerged to get even with those who had collaborated with the Russians.) Upon hearing that Lithuania was independent, many of the refugees wanted to escape from the Russian territories in Poland, especially when the news reached us that a Jewish organization, the American Joint Distribution Committee ("Joint" for short) was helping displaced people.

Some farmers who knew the territory organized illegal operations to smuggle people to Lithuania for money. It was dangerous because both the Russians and the Lithuanians reacted harshly against it. The borders were well guarded, especially on the Russian side. I toyed with the idea of going to Vilnius, formerly the Polish city of Wilno, which after the Russian occupation had become Lithuania's capital. I abandoned it after realizing that I could not speak Lithuanian, did not know anyone who lived there, did not have any money, and would not be allowed to work.

Then one day, unexpectedly, I received a letter, the first one I had received since the beginning of the war. My school friend Hela Znamirowska had learned my address from a mutual acquaintance who had previously escaped from Łuck to Vilnius. She suggested that I, too, come there, as conditions were much better than those in the Russian-occupied territories. A small colony of people from my hometown was also living there, having escaped at the start of the war. Hela lived in Vilnius with her parents and younger sister, whom I also knew from high school. (Her family had owned a flour mill and large lumber mill on the outskirts of Kalisz.) Her letter convinced me to escape to Vilnius. I quietly contacted people who were organizing a smuggling operation. They knew the terrain and the routes across it well. It was inadvisable to use any roads. As it was winter, the best way to move was across fields and woods when snow was falling, erasing one's tracks. I had read about the winters in the east and had seen them depicted in movies; but I could not imagine how severe they really were.

My work partner, Leon, had no urge to try the unknown, though he said he might go to Vilnius later. That later never came, and, after the German invasion of Lithuania in June, 1941, I never heard from him. He must have escaped to Russia and perished there or have been killed by the invading Germans, as were most of the Jews in Łuck. I never did find anyone who knew him or his fate. I suspect that, had I stayed in Łuck, I would have shared it.

My departure had to be arranged in total secrecy. Even my landlady couldn't know. We arranged that, when I did not return one evening, Leon would "worry" out loud that I had been arrested by the NKVD. No one would trace someone else in that situation for fear of being arrested oneself. And "undesirables" were shipped to Siberia to make room for the Russians moving west.

Joseph Stevens

I was advised that the best time to cross the Russian border would be at midnight on December 31st. At that time the Russians — especially the soldiers — would be celebrating the New Year with lots of vodka, music, and singing. The border patrols would be ineffectual. As it turned out, this was the case. On an otherwise quiet, snowy night we could easily hear their drunken noisemaking and bypass unsafe areas. Our guides assured us that the patrols did not use dogs. I was also told that the people with whom I had made the arrangements could be trusted.

Stories circulated that the "guides," as they called themselves, after receiving their money would abandon refugees in the woods or turn them over to the Russian border patrols, or worse. But an acquaintance recommended my guide to me. So, on December 30th, I went to his house and from there we went to a farmer's hut outside the city. To avoid suspicion, I did not carry anything with me. I was dressed as a worker, but with all the warm clothing I wore underneath I could hardly walk. My acquaintance introduced me to the farmer, and from then on I was at the mercy of a complete stranger. I removed some layers of clothing and waited until another fellow with the same destination appeared. We didn't talk much, feeling that in case of a disaster it was better that the other party knew as little as possible. I believe that this was an effect of the Communist regime, under which people feared and mistrusted each other.

That evening we were served soup and farmers bread, which tasted quite good. The three of us then dressed for the trip and left in a sleigh filled with straw. Some dirty blankets were available to cover our feet. A large, swift, well-kept horse pulled us along. We were warned to keep quiet under any circumstance.

Good Morning

I had paid half of the money for this trip to the acquaintance who made the arrangements and half to my working friend Leon, who was to pay the rest upon receiving word that I was safely in Vilnius. Half, in this case, did not mean half the amount, but half of the actual bills, which we had torn in two. I also had a note which I would finish on arriving in Vilnius and give to the "guide" who would take it back to Łuck to trade for the other halves of the banknotes.

The night was bright. With the white snow on the ground, no lamps were needed — not that we had any. We made good progress to the north, and it wasn't long before we started to feel the biting cold. The guide suggested that we get off the sleigh, hold onto the back, and run along behind. We quickly warmed up and jumped back on. The driver did the same. Running in my heavy clothing had made me tired and sweaty, so I became cold again. But this was still the best way to avoid freezing. With all my precautions and efforts, I still had to have two toes treated in Vilnius for frostbite. I was lucky that they didn't have to be amputated.

Well into the snowy second day, we arrived at another farmer's hut. He was expecting us. After we ate and relaxed a little inside, our first guide returned home, leaving us with the new guide to continue our trip on an identical sled with another fine horse. It became so cold that we could hear the snow crackling under our feet. Around our mouths our breath turned to ice and white hoarfrost covered our clothing. In the distance we could see lights and hear the Russians celebrating.

We were told when we approached the border area that we should remain completely quiet. Around us were only trees and a very large amount of snow, though I couldn't tell how high it actually was. It was exciting, but the most frightening experience of my life to that point. I knew the grave consequences should I be caught illegally crossing the border into Lithuania. I did not even have anything with me that I could use to bribe a guard. We shivered, whether more from cold or from fear I no longer remember.

Finally, we crossed into Lithuania. It didn't mean we were completely safe, though. Until they unloaded me at my destination I did not really believe I was in Vilnius. I gave my note to the guide, and he left. The city was very quiet because it was New Year's Day. When I arrived at the second floor of 16/18 Pohulanka Boulevard, the Znamirowski family was surprised to see me. First, I took a warm bath; then after a hot meal I was able to relax a little.

That afternoon Hela took me to Professor Liebert. He had been my high school Latin teacher for four years. He lived alone in an apartment with enough room for another person. He put me up nights, until I found a room for myself. Professor Liebert's wife and daughter had gone to visit her parents just before the outbreak of the war. They had been unable to return home and lost contact with him. As Hela and I walked to his apartment, I noticed it was so cold that I could hear the snow crunching under my feet on the sidewalk.

The following day I registered myself with the Lithuanian police as a refugee. At noon we ate at a restaurant which was run by the "Joint." The day after that I noticed that two toes on my right foot were white and had lost all feeling, except for itching. Hela took me to a hospital where I spent four days for frostbite. She also brought food to the hospital because none was provided.

Good Morning

The room I found was a shabby basement apartment in an old part of town belonging to a very old, poor woman. I began to awaken in the mornings with a splitting headache, which I attributed to the change in my life and the overall conditions. One day, Hela came to visit and found me still in bed. My mind was in a haze, and I had no motivation to do anything. She forced me to go to the hospital where I was diagnosed with carbon monoxide poisoning from the leaky old-fashioned iron stove with a big, black pipe vented out to the back yard. I was released the next day, after which I moved to a nice room with two new friends.

I had enrolled myself in a free vocational school supported by the "ORT" organization, so at first my life in Vilnius passed by uneventfully. I took courses in industrial electricity, food chemistry, and cosmetics production. My roommates also took some courses. They decided to use what they had been learning and started a business to produce essences for cold drinks to be sold to small stores. Our room looked like a laboratory and had a strong odor of many fragrances, as did our clothing. Eventually my roommates had the opportunity to emigrate. I helped produce documents for them that enabled them to leave "legally." (I recently learned that one of them has died, but the other still lives with his family in Los Angeles.)

Vilnius, which had been under Polish rule since 1920 (as Wilno), changed hands four times during the war. In October, 1939, the city had been transferred to Lithuania, a day marked by anti-Jewish riots. Many Jews were injured, and some deaths were reported. Later, the number of injured grew to the hundreds, as Jewish-owned shops and stores were vandalized and ransacked. The riots started with rumors that Jews were the cause of the soaring food prices, short supplies, and long lines at stores. Other rumors then spread that the Jews had killed a Catholic priest and a child. The Jewish leadership tried, unsuccessfully, to get the Lithuanian government to intervene. They were later more successful with the Russian administration in Vilnius. It dispatched tanks to restore order, but even they could not prevent sporadic fights between Polish and Lithuanian anti-Semites and Jews.

Eventually in early 1940, the Lithuanian militia was able to bring order to the streets. After further disturbances, the Jewish population received permission from the Lithuanian government to organize self-defense units. These groups received weapons but were under pressure from the Russians to obey the orders of the Lithuanian government. The situation eased, and the weapons became superfluous. The city filled with refugees from all elements of society: criminals released from Polish jails and other shady characters, families, young people, intellectuals, and some who had formerly held high positions. New businesses, local farmers, and professional smugglers flourished.

Some members of charitable and Jewish organizations risked their lives trying to help more people escape from the German-occupied territories across the Lithuanian border. Many never reached Vilnius but were caught by the Germans and killed on the spot. The Russian-Lithuanian border, on the other hand, was the territory of the professional smuggler. Refugees caught by the Russians were, if lucky, merely returned; but most were arrested and shipped to Siberia, where cold and hunger killed many. Other refugees, after paying their professional "guides," were abandoned by them in the middle of nowhere to freeze to death. The poor were turned over to Russian authorities. The lucky ones who reached Vilnius suffered from frostbite, and some died of gangrene or other complications. But they continued to come. Vilnius became so full of refugees that the Lithuanian government began to force them into other Lithuanian cities.

Then, on June 15, 1940, everything changed. The Russians entered Vilnius and installed a Communist regime, making Lithuania one of the Soviet Republics, as they did in Latvia and Estonia. This, of course, was at "the people's request." I again found myself living under Communist rule. They took charge immediately — nationalizing private industry, making the usual arrests, and proclaiming "*Nie robotsash, nie kutshash*" — "If you don't work, you don't eat." They claimed that unemployment did not exist under communism, so everybody could find a job. Only the bourgeois element did not want to work. They were parasites, enemies of the nation, enemies of the working class. The Communists created many projects from day to day, so that people could find "employment."

A new road suddenly needed to be built, requiring thousands of people because no mechanical equipment was available. Thousands of cubic yards of dirt had to be dug out of a mountain by hand and moved by wheelbarrow to human-powered carts that ran on flimsy, bent rails. These hand-wagons often derailed and the shoulders of many strong men had to lift them back on. When enough dirt had accumulated in one place the rails were moved a few yards to one side. I was on a team of four that loaded hand-wagons. We had to work quickly, as we were paid by the unit. The empty hand-wagons could not wait long, and we did not want to be penalized for not meeting our quota. A team that did not fill a minimum number of hand-wagons received less pay per unit; if they failed badly, they would be fired for sabotaging the work. We had to bring our own shovels. Each hour of work became harder and harder. By the end of the day I could hardly move. The next morning I didn't go to work because I could not get up from bed; not a muscle in my body didn't ache. This was the end of my career as a road builder.

Fortunately, an acquaintance of Hela's father knew a building engineer who was in charge of some large projects. One of them was a big building where all of the newly nationalized graphic industry plants were being transferred. At that time, to get a good job you had to be a Communist or know someone important, not necessarily be qualified for the work. By a stroke of fortune, Henry Katcherginsky, the engineer, sent me to work on the project as an assistant to the chief architect. From the moment we met, I struck a personal bond with the architect. We trusted each other, though generally we did not reveal much about ourselves; it was too dangerous. I thought the architect was no friend of the Communists, but who could know? The longer we worked together, the more we built trust and confidence in each other. He hated the Lithuanians, the Russians, and the Communists.

He asked me to prepare the plans for a section. I drew what I thought were good plans with all the specifications. After looking at my finished plans for a long time, he looked me straight in the eye and said that I had never studied architecture; the plans were good, but they were not professionally rendered. I admitted the truth. He gave me some instructions and hints. In retrospect, I realize I also gave him hints about the graphic arts industry. We helped each other whenever we could, developing a sincere mutual friendship and deep confidence in each other. We covered up irregularities so the other wouldn't get into trouble, which would have been easy since the building was for the Communist Ministry of Information and Propaganda.

Shortages of building materials were commonplace because they were in short supply. But requisitions on our official letterhead worked like magic, giving us priority for everything we needed. Still, all the scaffolding and supports for workers were built out of wood. The outside steps and the ramps for the wheelbarrows were improvised. Hardly any mechanical equipment was available. Even in the 1940s this was considered primitive.

Small tools like hammers, saws, and pliers were stored in one of the rooms. Before long they started to disappear. I came up with a suggestion, which management considered a "great idea." The man in charge of inventory was made responsible for all the tools. He was supposed to hang all the tools on the wall, with an outline drawn on the wall for each. Each worker was given a number which, upon taking a tool, was placed on the hook in its place. The system worked for a while; but when the end-of-the-workday whistle sounded, workers in their impatience to leave just dumped the tools in a pile.

CHAPTER THREE

৵৶

Most of the refugees from the western countries became discouraged with the political situation. Stagnant circumstances and an uncertain future created tension and nervousness among all. The only solution was to emigrate, but how, and to where? It was almost impossible to leave the Russian-occupied territories legally. In Kaunas, the previous capital of Lithuania, some embassies, consulates, and official envoys were still active. People tried to obtain false passports or visas to distant countries — to Turkey, or via Curaçao to Japan, anywhere far from the Russians and Germans. They would use any means they could and pay large bribes. To travel outside the country one had to go through Moscow by train. Arrangements had to be made through the state-owned Russian Travel Bureau, the only one allowed. The only hotel for foreigners, "Intourist" (which was also state-owned and managed by the travel bureau), was very expensive. The only legal way to pay for the travel and hotel was to have someone from a country outside of Russian control pay for it in dollars. Another difficult task was to obtain an exit visa from the Russians. In their view, anyone who wanted to leave the Communist "haven" was suspect and should be investigated by the NKVD, the Communist political secret police. It controlled all areas of life in Russia and the occupied countries and wanted to know what contacts potential emigrants had abroad, who had paid for their travel, if the money might have come from an account of their own somewhere in the free world, what relation they had to the people who had paid, their entire life history. No detail was left unquestioned. Some people were called back several times for more questioning. Some were arrested. Some were sent to Siberia. One never knew when one might be called to receive an exit visa, a rejection, or something worse.

Some young people were able to emigrate under the pretext of going abroad to study. One could enroll at the university in Haifa or another city in Palestine, then under British mandate; but it was necessary to have a high school diploma and mail it to someone who would enroll the candidate by paying for one semester in advance. Some people I knew emigrated that way. They did not have their high school diplomas with them, because who thought of unimportant things like that while escaping from the Germans? I was able to help them by printing "original" documents. (I learned after the war that one of them, whose name was Colton, ended up living with his family in Los Angeles. Another, Almagor, became an attorney, practicing law in Tel Aviv. Eventually he served as Israeli ambassador to Poland and later to Chile.) I also was able to help some people with visas. I had some originals that I could reproduce. One man with a family bought a foreign passport with his last money, but the photograph with the seal and the name had to be changed. I impressed even myself with the results. The changes were barely detectable. Though I could have submitted any of the necessary documents for myself, I was not lucky enough to have someone enroll me in a university.

Another big change occurred when the Znamirowski

family received an exit visa. Again, I was losing a home where I had been accepted as one of the family. Every day after work I would visit, and Hela would be waiting with dinner. I could turn to her father for financial help or to her mother for any other assistance. We went on the train together as far as Kaunas. My good-bye to Hela and her family was not an easy one. They continued on to Moscow, staying in the foreigners-only Intourist hotel, waiting for a chance to board a train to Kiev on the way to Messina. Each night for more than a week I went to the post office, the only place where one could place a long-distance call to Moscow. Each night I waited many long hours for the clerk to tell me my call was ready, but I could never get a connection. I lost contact with them until after the war.

While I didn't have valid documents for travel abroad, I applied for an exit visa, hoping that something would turn up. One day I went to the NKVD office to inquire about my case and was arrested on the spot. I did not know why. In the cell I was convinced that this was the end of my freedom. There was no place to wash or sleep. The concrete floor and walls were dirty and hard; the only "decoration" was a small light bulb hanging from a short wire. Once a day I was fed watery potato soup and a piece of bread. The only bright spot was that I was dressed warmly. I had no opportunity to learn why I had been arrested, but I knew that in every cell there was one "prisoner" who was an informer. I loudly complained that I couldn't understand why I had been arrested: a model citizen, a poor man who had worked hard all his life, with parents who were also very poor and descended from a working family, someone who liked Communists, and so on. I always complained loudly so that everyone could hear me. Some did not like my political views, but in that situation I didn't care. I trusted no one.

On the third day my name was called — I was certain for interrogation, but I wanted finally to learn what was going on. I was led to a room where a uniformed man sitting behind a wooden table returned my documents and told me that I could go home. I did not dare to ask why I had been jailed, because that was not proper behavior under the Communist regime. I also didn't ask for my watch and belt to be returned.

The first thing I did upon arriving home was scrub myself from a pan of warm water and soap. I did not have a shower or access to a tub. The next day, when I returned to work, nobody could believe that I had been freed so quickly. I started work but feared that I would soon be arrested again. This was not unusual.

The uncertain days passed uneventfully. A growing number of people came to the construction site looking for work. One man said that he was a bookkeeper, capable of doing paperwork or anything that was necessary. He was desperate because his wife was ill and unable to work, and he needed food for his family. The architect who was in charge of hiring rejected him as there really wasn't an opening for his kind of work. We did all of the office work ourselves. I noticed tears in the man's eyes as he left. I followed because I felt he was a refined man, decent and in distress. We had a brief chat and from that moment developed a mutual trust in each other. He confessed in deep secrecy that before the war he had been a professional officer and bookkeeper at the garrison in Wilno. The Communists were hunting him, as they were all former officers of the army. He gave me his real name, Właldysław Rzadkowski, and told me where he lived on

Mickiewicza Street. I told him that I would do whatever I could.

I bought some food, wearing dirty working overalls to avoid suspicion, and put it into a sack that I carried on my shoulder. Two days later I went to his apartment and asked for him. I scared his family greatly. They told me that he had abandoned them some time ago, that they didn't know what had happened to him or where he was. After I introduced myself, I explained the circumstances under which we had met, that my clothing was just a disguise, and that I had brought some food for them. They still had some doubts about me, they told me later, because the story sounded too simple to believe and too good to be true. Finally they admitted that Wladyslaw had gone to the country to obtain some food, as many did, and was supposed to return in two days. In the meantime, I talked to the architect and described the situation. He agreed that Właldysław could help us with the paperwork but would be registered as a worker. Two days later, when I returned to the Rzadkowski family and brought some more food, they could not thank me enough. The next day he started working, and we developed a close friendship.

As the months passed, my main concern was to avoid being arrested by the Russians. I had been leading a quiet life and tried to be in contact with as few people as possible, especially those whom I did not know well. I gave up my dream of emigrating. Escaping illegally seemed impossible, and I did not know where I might go. But in June 1941 the bubble burst. The non-aggression pact of 1939 between Hitler and Stalin proved, as everyone expected, to be a temporary convenience. Nazi Germany invaded Russia under the pretext of liberating the world from Communists, Bolsheviks, and Jews.

In the middle of a quiet Sunday morning on June 22nd the sirens sounded in Vilnius. I heard explosions in the distance which I assumed were part of some Russian drills. But when I went for a walk later, I saw excitement and commotion in the streets. Curious, I asked around and heard about a radio announcement: the Germans had attacked and invaded Russian territory. As I returned home, I again heard explosions: not drills, but German planes dropping bombs. That evening there were more — still closer.

Panic overwhelmed Vilnius. All the Russians packed whatever they could and escaped to the east. Most of the families of Russian military and office personnel loaded whatever trunks they had and confiscated any working vehicles. They hated to part with all the booty, including furniture, which they had previously collected, and were saddened to leave their luxurious living quarters. The Lithuanians and Poles who had collaborated with the Communists also tried to escape to Russia, as did many Jews, fearing the consequences of having to live under the Nazi regime.

There were rumors that some of the railroad trains transporting escapees had been bombed by the Germans. I saw horse-drawn wagons carrying Jewish families and some of their belongings. Many people were frightened and confused, not knowing what to do. We knew that the front line was rapidly moving in our direction when we saw masses of evacuees from the western part of Lithuania moving east through the city. It became obvious that the Russian army was retreating when large numbers of soldiers and military equipment also passed through towards the east. The Russians told people that this was only a temporary, strategic retreat for regrouping.

I also saw a few individual Russian planes (never in any formation) heading toward the front lines, but I never saw any returning. They were nicknamed "flying Russian cows" because of their slowness and fat unmaneuverable appearance. I heard that they were easy targets for the German anti-aircraft artillery and no match for the Luftwaffe. A day before the Germans marched into Vilnius, I saw one of the slow-moving Russian planes over the city. A German plane approached it and quickly shot it down.

In the general panic and confusion I couldn't decide what to do. By waiting for the Germans, I would again be under Nazi rule, something I had struggled to avoid. On the other hand, to try to escape east would expose me to the Communist terror inside Russia and eventually lead to my being shipped to Siberia as an undesirable.

But before I could make up my mind, just two days after the invasion on June 24, 1941, the Germans occupied Vilnius. I found myself living under Nazi occupation, but under different circumstances than those in Vienna. This time I couldn't wear an "Ausländer" (foreigner) badge. In Vienna the Nazis had still respected the nationals of the countries which they hadn't yet invaded. Now I was a Jew, a person they had come to destroy, and it made no difference where I was a citizen. Moreover, the invading Germans had the help of many Lithuanians who were proud to collaborate with them and who considered the Nazis their liberators and friends. I was nauseated to see Lithuanians greeting the German troops marching in.

From the beginning, all administration was organized

under Lithuanian-German leadership. This changed later when the Germans took over most civilian offices, including the Lithuanian militia and other law enforcement agencies, using them as they pleased. (On the other hand, the Lithuanians were eager to execute the dirty duties they were assigned.) All announcements and public orders were made only with the permission of the German Military Administration. The official currency became the German Reichsmark, although the ruble was still in circulation.

All Jews were soon required to wear armbands with yellow stars, visible to all. The German edict, posted everywhere, specified the exact size of the star and how it should be worn. A letter "J" (for *Jude*: Jew) of a particular appearance and size had to be in the star's center. The moment I read the decree I decided to disobey it. Though the penalty for defying the order was death, I realized that wearing the star would lead to my end. Why expose myself to the additional humiliation?

It wasn't long before additional decrees were posted. Jews were forbidden from the main streets. Those who lived on them were required to go to the nearest intersection and use the side street. Jews were forbidden to walk on the sidewalks. Curfews were established. All these decrees carried the death penalty for disobeying them. Stores posted signs: "Off limits to dogs and Jews." In fact, all public places such as offices, hospitals, restaurants, theaters, even barber shops and the like were off limits. People were in disbelief, wondering what would happen next.

The Germans had no difficulty recruiting eager collaborators. Lithuanian civilians, proudly wearing German armbands, cruised along the lines forming in front of the stores, fishing for undesirables. On spotting a Jew, they pulled him from the line, kicked and beat him, and often turned him over to the German authorities. They accused innocent people of being Bolsheviks or Communists in order to make a better impression on the Germans. They were proud to be able to spit on the people who were walking alongside the curb.

I knew, from what I had seen in Vienna, that life as a Jew would be unbearable. The conditions for Jews in Lithuania were even worse than what I had heard about in other occupied countries. My only option was to pretend not to be a Jew. If I was caught, which could happen at any time, I would be killed for that crime, perhaps tortured first, yet I walked on the sidewalk with my head up, impudent and brazen, to show that I was not afraid of anyone. My Aryan features and blond hair helped me in the masquerade; without them, I wouldn't have had a chance. But my heart pounded from the fear that someone would recognize me.

Then the orders came that all Jews had to move to the ghetto, the most dilapidated part of town. I decided that I would prefer to die than move there. I had heard about the conditions and atrocities in other ghettos and was convinced that I would perish one way or another. Staying in Vilnius and hiding, for however long, wasn't an option. I didn't know anyone who would risk his own and his family's life hiding me, especially since I didn't have dollars, gold, diamonds, or other riches to persuade them. No, I couldn't stay in Vilnius at all, because eventually someone would recognize me and turn me over to the Germans. That would earn a reward of four kilos of sugar or flour.

By coincidence—more like a miracle—I learned from Mr. Rzadkowski of a farmer who was looking for a hand who knew German and could teach it to his son and daughter. He lived on a small farm in a village named Rukojnie, not far from Vilnius. Before the war he had also been the village postmaster. His duties were to distribute the few letters that were delivered to him from Vilnius to the other farmers. (This was a prestigious position because he was respected by the villagers for being able to read and write.) In desperation I decided to try for the job. I told the people from whom I rented a room that I was moving into the ghetto, but I went in another direction.

Some city people went to the country to buy or barter for produce, which was as scarce in the city as any other food. I pretended to do the same. I took with me some "clean" documents, which didn't identify me as Jewish, and a very small bundle, so as not to arouse anyone's suspicions. I told my landlady that I would pick up my winter clothing and other belongings later, when I was allowed to leave the ghetto. Otherwise, she could sell them or give them to someone. She understood my decision as discouragement and that I considered my position hopeless.

I walked to Rukojnie, taking the side roads to avoid German sentries. I worried only about what I might do if I did not get the job on the farm. Upon finally reaching the village, I had no trouble locating the farmer: everyone knew the "postmaster." When I introduced myself as an experienced farmhand, I noticed that he glanced at my hands and smiled to himself. I immediately told him that my father had a farm and that I had worked there only during my school and college vacations. I told him I would be a valuable farmhand because I liked that kind of work. I knew the German language well and I didn't hide that I had studied in Vienna. He was impressed, not knowing of any farmhands who had attended a university. He was proud to have me teach his children, teenagers who had hardly any education.

The farmer told me where I would sleep: on a straw sack next to the oven. I started work immediately for room and board. To avoid suspicion I imitated his son, who always worked with me. I complained that I was not strong because I had been living in the city. The second day I was sore all over, but I didn't let it show. My hands were blistered so badly that I had to wrap them in rags. Soon, I learned how to lift and throw heavy sacks of potatoes, grain, and vegetables onto my back and carry them on my shoulders without difficulty.

On Sunday, the farmer let me go with his family to the church. Everyone went, except for his son, who had to take care of the livestock. It was a Catholic church, the only parish in the area. Everyone in Rukojnie was Catholic when I got there. But there was supposed to have been one poor Jewish family — until the German invasion. The village bailiff denounced them to the Germans, and they were taken away, never to be heard of again. The bailiff confiscated their hut and their land, which made the other villagers envious. The wife of the farmer who hired me thought that the family was a mixture of Jewish and Lutheran, having seen one of the sons with a Lutheran bible. Not wanting to show any unusual interest in the subject, I let it drop and never learned any more. No other Jewish family lived there or in the surrounding villages.

As a small boy I had a nanny who was a devoted Catholic. Most Sundays she attended the Kanoników church in Kalisz. I liked to accompany her there to see the church service. I especially liked the performances of the altar boys. I envied their marching in the procession dressed in fancy white robes. They carried holy figures mounted on sticks that were decorated with crosses and many small jingling bells. They extinguished the candles with their long candle snuffers and performed all kinds of activities in assisting the priests. I wanted to become one of them someday just as other little boys might want to become a fireman or policeman. I never imagined that my experience would someday enable me to pass as a Catholic.

Although I hadn't attended a Catholic service for many years I felt comfortable and sure of myself in the church. I remembered most of the prayers. I knew when to kneel, when to cross myself, and when to bow my head. When I wasn't certain I imitated the others. No one could tell I wasn't a religious, practicing Catholic.

The older priest, Michael Michnowicz, pastor of Parish Rukojnie, learned from the farmer who had hired me what I was doing in the village and that I knew German. There were not many people living there, and everyone knew everyone else. It was not difficult for the priest to detect a newcomer. That same Sunday he invited himself for refreshments at the farmer's house. It was an honor for the family to have the priest visit.

Knowing that I knew German, the visiting priest asked if I would be willing to help with a problem. He wanted to petition the German authorities in Vilnius for the denationalization of some church properties. (The occupying Germans had left issues with the Church on hold, because they had to attend to "more important" matters.) He requested my help as a translator, suggesting that we go together the next day, Monday. He also asked where and to which office we should go. I knew as little as he did but, wanting to show my knowledge, told him that we should approach the civilian administration of the territories. The only way to check this would be to go to Vilnius to investigate. As soon as I said it I realized that I was putting my head into the lion's mouth, that cruising around Vilnius, where I might be recognized, would be very dangerous. I didn't have any way to withdraw my offer though. I told him that I would be glad to go with him, that it would be an honor to do this for the parish, as I had no money or other resources. (The farmers paid the priests mostly in farm products. I noticed that when they came to church or to confession they always brought eggs, flour, bread, cheese, or even a live chicken in their baskets.)

But the next morning, instead of the priest coming to pick me up in his black two-wheeled carriage, only his coachman arrived. He said that the priest felt sick and wondered if I would be willing to go alone as his representative. With the priest in his black cassock I would have had a distraction. Alone I would be exposed to much more danger. Not seeing an alternative to the predicament in which I had placed myself, I got into the carriage without hesitation, and we drove to Vilnius. Luckily, no one stopped us on the way to find out who we were or to check our documents.

Once in Vilnius, I did not know where to start. I made some inquiries and arrived at a German-Lithuanian administration building. I expected it to be a civilian office, but the armed sentry out front would not let me in without a pass. He sent me to another guard who, after considerable persuasion, let me enter. I noticed a sign for the secretariat and thought that it might be the right place. On a subconscious level I worked up a sense of assertiveness. I knocked on the door and walked in. There was a German officer sitting behind a desk who looked surprised when he noticed me. In the corner sat a chic blonde secretary typing rapidly on a manual typewriter. I clicked my heels together as German soldiers did when saluting. I immediately came to the point and explained why I was there. After I finished, the officer shouted at me, "You know we are now at war with the Russians. We have more important things to do. We don't have time for such pitiful and trifling matters now!"

Never before had I pounded on someone's desk or table, so it is difficult for me to comprehend what I did then: I put my fist on his desk. His face turned red and I almost expected him to take his revolver from his holster. I had created a situation that he considered confrontational. Before he could say or do something that I would regret, I said, "If I return to Rukojnie empty-handed they will call me a Communist. I can't go back. If I tell them what happened they will wonder why you are accepting things which the Communist Bolsheviks did. Please, help me, because I am afraid to return."

I don't know what ran through his mind. I think my flawless German must have helped, because there weren't many non-Germans in the territories who were able to speak that well. (I had told him earlier, in answer to his question, about my five years of high school German and my studies in Vienna during the Anschluss). He cooled off, and after a moment asked, "So, what do you want?"

I replied, very politely, that I wanted a document that certified that all the church property in Rukojnie nationalized by the Communists should be returned. I knew that the Nazis were not fond of the Catholic Church, although many Catholics were collaborating with them. The officer dictated something to his secretary. When she returned, he read it, stamped it (his stamp included a large swastika), signed the original, and threw it on the desk for me to pick up. In response to my thanks for his justice, he replied, "I don't ever want to see you again—or your priest."

I assured him I would never be back, simultaneously saluting and again clicking the heels of my heavy shoes. My entry had been slow and uncertain, but my exit was swift and sure. I had to pull myself together because I didn't believe what I had just done.

I found the coachman in the courtyard of the apartment house where we had parked and we started home. I didn't worry about not having identification, because I felt the document I carried would get us through any checkpoint. I took the document out to analyze what it said and had a shock when I saw an old printed Lithuanian form. Then I turned it over and calmed down. The Germans hadn't wasted any paper that was used only on one side. I first saw the large seal with the swastika. Anything stamped with a swastika worked like magic in Lithuanian civilian offices. I was pleased, convinced that this document was what we wanted. On the other hand, I had some doubts that a denationalization could be processed on the basis of such a simple paper. The return trip passed uneventfully, but I had learned an important principle: never look down or appear scared. This immediately creates suspicion in others. Stand straight and look them right in the eyes, making your case before they have a chance to interrogate you. Unfortunately, this did not always work, as I found out later.

I gave the document to the priest and translated it for him. He called in his young curate, the vicar of the parish, Michael (Witold) Szymczukiewicz, and the organist, Antoni Lobacz, and showed it to the two of them in turn.

He thanked me, blessed me, and called it a miracle. They smiled with disbelief at what I had accomplished. The priest then asked me what they should do with the document. I told him that I thought the right thing to do was to take it to the Lithuanian authorities that administered the territories along with the Germans. The priest could not speak any Lithuanian and asked me if I would be so kind as to arrange this for him. I was dumbfounded. Again I had involved myself in a dangerous situation.

The next day I learned from the farmers that the bailiff was in charge. When I started to explain to him the purpose of my visit and showed him the document with the swastika, he became scared, not knowing who I was or what the document said. I translated it to him in my poor Lithuanian, and then went on the offensive. My brief experience had taught me that one achieved the best results by putting the other party on the defensive, not only giving one a better position but also eliminating any trace of suspicion. I insisted that it was his duty to send the militia to the peasants on the church's land, to inform them that the land which the Communists gave them no longer belonged to them. They would have to return it to the church or lease it from the church as they had done before it was nationalized. The bailiff also had to ensure that the change was entered into the permanent records in the proper office.

Actually, I didn't know if what I was saying was correct; I was improvising. The bailiff said he would comply, but that he didn't know when. I responded that all of it had to be done the very next day, or I would report him to the German authorities. (I was sure that he collaborated with the Germans, because he could not otherwise have obtained his position.) He agreed to the demands. Then he asked to keep the document. I told him that the document belonged to the priest but that I could make a copy for him. I did the secretarial work using a pencil and piece of paper that he provided. He kept his part of the deal, as the next day the farmers came to the priest begging for forgiveness. I did not learn whether the change was made to the records book.

At the following Sunday's church service, near the end of the sermon, the senior priest said, "We have in our parish a newcomer who has done more for the parish than all of you sinners." He pointed in my direction. I was sitting in the back of the church, but all of the faces suddenly turned to look at me. I wished I could bury my head in the sand, like an ostrich. I was so embarrassed that I didn't know what to do with myself. From that moment I became a saint in the village. All doors were open for me; everyone wanted my company. I was supposed to have answers to all the poor farmer's questions and problems — except in farming.

I also became a close friend of the church organist, who lived at the parish house. We discussed all kinds of topics. He enjoyed my company and told me a lot about himself. Naturally, I told him about myself in return, but only the things I wanted him to know. I would talk about myself, with certainty and conviction, but not about anything that might identify my religion. I tried not to lie, so as not to forget the next time what I had made up. I did not want to lose the credibility and trust the people had in me. Sometimes, though, I caught myself in exaggerations, mainly when I thought someone was suspicious of me.

Given my close relations with the church, nobody suspected I was not Catholic. I impressed even the priest with my grasp of Latin, the product of four years' lessons in high school. At that time some of the prayers were recited or repeated after the priest, in Latin, but people did not understand what they were saying. At one point the senior priest asked me if I would help with the catechism, promising me that I would be blessed if I taught the young children on Sundays. I immediately agreed, having no idea what I was supposed to do. I asked him for some direction, and he handed me a very old, worn-out book to read. It was easier for me to perform than I thought it would be. I just repeated the material to the children without any additions or interpretations of my own, despite my reservations about the text. As it wasn't customary for the children to ask any questions, I did not find myself in any embarrassing positions.

One day, as I was walking out of the hut in which I lived, I saw a strange man approaching. He was tall and held himself very straight. It was clear from first glance that he was a city man. I thought he was coming to the village to purchase some farm products. He walked up to me and asked if I knew a fellow who had recently come from town, who knew German, whose name was Józef Szczecinski, and where to find him. I said, "That's me." He raised his eyebrows slightly as if surprised. Perhaps he thought I would be dressed differently than in barn-caked boots and dusty shirt, like a typical peasant.

He said he wanted to talk to me. I answered, "We can talk right here." He preferred to talk inside, in private. I lifted my head in surprise and in a confident voice said, "I don't have any secrets, do you?" A thousand thoughts went through my mind in that instant. What did a total stranger want from me, and why did he want to talk in private? Had he learned I was Jewish and wanted to blackmail me? The practice was common enough. Though I thought I was facing a death sentence, I didn't let it show from my expression. I had no wealth, and my clothing would not satisfy him. He would get more from the Germans for informing on me: some sugar, flour, and perhaps some whiskey.

We walked into the hut and sat down on a wooden bench. He looked around to be sure that no one had accompanied us and asked if anyone could hear us. With a firm but low voice he introduced himself as an officer of the Polish National Army (the Armia Krajowa). He said that he knew for a fact that I was also an officer, and that he had come to induct me into the Underground. Instantly, my thoughts turned 180 degrees in disbelief and relief.

Earlier, I would have given anything, as would have many others, to have had an opportunity to join the Resistance instead of being hunted. But the only partisans that Jews could join were the People's Army (Armia Ludowa), which was controlled by the Soviet government. The National Army did not accept any Jews. On the contrary, they considered Jews to be their enemies.

Looking the man straight in the eye, I denied everything that he said about me. I told him that I was too young to have been an officer and had never served in any army. I had always been ill and a weakling and had been rejected by the Military Medical Commission. But he said that he knew all about my military history and started to rattle off facts that I immediately realized only one person of my present acquaintance knew: the church organist. He was the only person who showed interest in my past, and I had confided in him because I trusted him. I also realized that he must have been a member of the Underground, though it was a long time before I discussed that dangerous subject with him. Though he was not physically strong and was of poor build, he often talked to me about the military resistance. He was a very convincing chauvinist, hating Germans, Russians, Lithuanians, Jews, and anyone else who was not Polish.

Nonetheless, I told the officer that everything he said was untrue, and that I did not know where he had gotten his information, especially the part about my being new here and not having many acquaintances. I added that perhaps he was a German collaborator who was looking for innocent people to get into trouble. Besides, he didn't have any credentials. At that, he reached into his back pocket and took out a small revolver, saying, "Here are my credentials." I told him that while his information about me wasn't true, I would have to admit that I was at his mercy without a revolver of my own. And even if I'd had one, I wouldn't have known how to use it. He answered that he liked my approach and that I was the kind of person who was very much in demand in the Army.

He rose from the bench and took a crucifix from the wall. (The custom of the village was that every room had a crucifix or holy picture hanging in it.) He placed it on the table, put his gun on top of it and my hand on top of both. He told me to repeat an oath after him: "In the name of the Father, the Son, and the Holy Ghost . . ." I do not remember the exact words, but in essence I swore obedience to the National Army; to fight, without regard to my personal safety, until victory; to always obey the orders of my superiors without hesitation; and to never reveal the identity of my comrades or the secrets entrusted to me; all under penalty of death without a court martial.

He took my hand off the gun and gave it to me, saying that from now on it was mine; to guard it, and use it when necessary. He told me to choose a pseudonym because my real name would never be used in the army for security reasons. I was supposed to report in Vilnius where I would receive further orders. All the information was to be kept confidential and nothing was to be written down. Every instruction and every detail had to be memorized.

When I arrived at a certain address in Vilnius, he told me, I would find myself in front of a small shop selling all sorts of new and used items for which people had little use, even during the war—in other words, junk. If I noticed a white object in one corner of the window I should enter. On the other hand, if it was not there, I should walk on past the store as if I had never intended to go in. I should never look around to see if someone was watching me; instead I should look out of the corner of my eye to see if anything looked unusual or suspicious. I should never change my pace or run. Since I did not have anything with me that might compromise me, I would have nothing to be afraid of. If I was not to go in, I would be notified where and when I should come again.

Everything seemed okay on the day I marched to Vilnius, so I walked into the store according to the plan. If a customer was inside I was supposed to browse disinterestedly. Once alone with the clerk, I asked for a round box. He said he did not have one, and I replied that I should have asked for an oval one. Again, he said he did not have one, and I asked for a square one. He said that he did not have one of those either, but added, "I think I have just the right one for you. For what purpose do you need it?" That confirmed I was talking to the right man.

I told him my name was Szczupak (my new pseudonym, "pike"). He took me into an adjacent room after he closed and locked the store. He then came right to the point—I could take no notes and would have to memorize everything. My first order was to choose two people whom I could trust without question and induct them the same way I had been sworn in. I had to be completely convinced that I had chosen the right men in every respect. The safety of the organization, and my own, had to be guarded. No one should know about my affiliation with the Underground, except the two people I chose. Until the proper time. These two should not know about my contact in Vilnius. Later, those two would have to organize their own cells, which would have no contact with the other. This was necessary for security reasons. The Germans were cruel, and some people, if caught, could take only so much torture before revealing what and whom they knew.

I was also ordered to obtain any kind of weapon I could put my hands on. Supplies and air drops were too far east; so, for the time being, we had to depend on ourselves. I thought that it would be too complicated and risky using the one small handgun I had to steal more weapons from the Germans. And I did not have the contacts or resources with which to pay someone else for them.

The clerk suggested the following. He said that during the Russian-Polish battles in 1939 and the German-Russian battles in 1941, much armament had been left on the fields by the retreating armies. The poor peasant farmers who lived in those areas collected them, as they were made of iron. They hoped they might be able to forge farming tools from them.

From time to time, he also warned me, the Germans forcibly conscripted able-bodied men to serve in satellite units of the army, building roads or doing other heavy work. Some were shipped to Germany as farm or factory workers or to clean up the damage done by Allied forces.

To protect myself, I would have to change jobs. I would have to be in a position where I would have more freedom and where my every move would not be monitored. Indeed, my trip to Vilnius had not been taken well by my boss. I had to make all kinds of excuses to get out of working in the fields.

Arrangements had already been made for my "promotion." I would work in the same village, but on the Rukojnie Estate, the largest farm in Rukojnie. It also had fish hatcheries, over which I was to be officially in charge. In fact, I would work whenever the manager of the farm wanted me to work. They would also obtain from the German authorities an Unabkömlichkeit Bescheinigung, which declared me indispensable in civilian life and would protect me from being transferred anywhere. Once fish reached a given weight they were to be delivered to a depot for collection by the German army. Items such as gasoline and food had priorities that were set by the army. Their production was also controlled by the army, under threat of death.

My sudden change of status to that of an irreplaceable person for the German food industry made me feel like a VIP. However, my knowledge of fish was limited to that of a fillet ready to eat on my plate. I did not even know anything about fishing. It wasn't a sport at the time. I only remember some poor people fishing for food by the river. They used a tree branch, some string, and a worm on a hook.

I learned later that the Rukojnie Estate belonged, before the war, to the Polish general Takarzewski. When the Russians invaded that territory they had nationalized it. Then the Germans took it over from the Russians. The fellow who administered the land was Tadeusz Zaborski. He had a formal agricultural education but worked with us like a regular farmer. He used modern tools whenever they were available. The farmers in the village thought his practices were funny. I remember that he bought a few bags of fertilizer from some place in Vilnius and cast it by hand because we didn't have any spreaders. The farmers called it magic sand and didn't think it would do any good. The best fertilizer, according to them, came from the cow barn. That had worked for generations.

I moved into a farmhouse on the estate. It looked like a crude log cabin with a roof made of straw. All the huts in the village had looked the same to me: very primitive, only differing in size. This one had a room with a built-in oven that also served as the kitchen and bakery. Every few weeks bread was baked there. It was fresh, dark farmers bread, and, if we were lucky, it was served with a very small amount of butter. It tasted to me then like the best cake might taste today. The oven was so big that it had room for two people to sleep in it. Because it was warm, it was a privileged place reserved for the woman farmhand who helped in the household and cooked. My quarters were a small nook which I shared with two farmhands who later became my closest companions. I slept in a rough wooden bunk on a straw sack that served for a mattress. After a day's work, though, I could have slept well on the clay floor.

The wooden outhouse, built of rough boards, was placed well away from the hut. It was an important part of the complex whose precious cargo was emptied twice a year, in the spring and fall. It was loaded onto a wagon, spread on the fields, and plowed into the soil as fertilizer. It was considered improper to not pick up this "gold" with a shovel if it fell off the wagon on the way. I helped in the operation sometimes. While in the beginning I could not believe what I was doing, later it came as naturally as if I had been born to that kind of life.

The same operation was performed for the cows and sheep. The manure was collected from the barn twice a year. Every day, fresh straw was spread on the floor while the animals were outside. This preserved the manure and kept the cows clean when they lay down and chewed their cud. The horses were a different story. They normally stood unless they were sick. Their manure was used only on the field where onions were grown.

We joked that the barns grew taller after their semi-annual cleanings because we removed quite a few feet of deposits. The straw, being biodegradable, was hardly recognizable. We used biodegradable materials in the outhouse, too: old newspapers, if available; large fresh leaves picked up on the way out, or, in the winter, lots of snow. We didn't use the outhouse as much in the summer as we did in the winter. When working in the fields nobody bothered to waste time running all the way back. It was more convenient to use the field or to go behind some bushes. The winter nights were a problem though. Temperatures of –30° to –40°C were not uncommon, often accompanied by very strong winds and drifting snow. The hut and all the barns were built on a hill, the highest part of the land through which the wind whistled unbelievably, as in scenes from the movie *Dr. Zhivago*. Surprisingly, over the entire three years I lived on the farm, I never caught a cold, even though our clothing, food, and living conditions left much to be desired.

Tadeusz Zaborski, the administrator of the farms, (as I learned later) knew that I was involved in the Underground and therefore tolerated my absences. He taught me all he knew about artificial lakes and fish breeding, obtaining for me a German book on the subject, from which I translated some chapters I thought he would find important. I did this work in the evenings by the light of a kerosene or carbide lamp. During this time even kerosene and carbide were hard to obtain.

Our lakes and procedures were not as modern and sophisticated as those described in the book. Our feeding practices were nauseating. We suspended the unusable parts of chickens and other slaughtered animals on narrow boards above water level. When the mass decayed, a swarm of bugs and worms developed on and around it, falling into the water, to the delight of the fish. They were king carps, which will eat anything. A few male pikes were also placed in the lakes where somewhat larger fish were raised. They were supposed to hunt and chase the fish so they would not become torpid. The sick and weak were devoured by the pikes. We were then supposed to deliver the entire grown crop of fish to the special depot for the Germans.

I learned from the book what kinds of diseases could strike the fish, what kinds of mechanical disasters might happen, how a screen or dam might break and allow the fish to escape. Of course, how to prevent all those problems we always learned after the fact. We used all these excuses to explain why we were unable to deliver any fish to the depot (though we had for ourselves all the fish we wanted). We also knew that the farmers from the village were stealing fish from the ponds at night, but we pretended not to see what was going on.

The close acquaintance of the farm administrator and the area forester was highly beneficial for us. Wood, like every other commodity, was very scarce for the civilian population despite the forests in the vicinity. Thanks to our connection, when we received an allocation of wood from the German authorities, we could help ourselves to as much as we needed. Trees were the only material we had for building cabins, barns, or anything. Of course, we had to fell the trees ourselves, drag them out of the crowded forest, load them onto the horse-drawn wagon, and haul them home. I learned how to properly sharpen a hand saw and how to saw and chop thick trunks so that a tree would not fall in the wrong direction. When we were finally able to bring a load home, we could not ride with it. That would have made the load too heavy for the horses. Instead we sometimes even had to push to help the horses, such as when a wheel got stuck in a hole. There weren't any roads to speak of, only paths, sometimes muddy or sandy. The wagon we used was unusual. The front part with two wheels was hitched to the horses and supported one end of the trees. The separated rear part with the other two wheels supported the other end of the trees and was tied to them. It made me uncomfortable to see how hard the horses were working, with steam rising from their bodies, big horseflies constantly bothering them, and the coachman mercilessly using his whip.

When a load of trees was brought in we had to sort them and chop off the branches with axes. Those logs were the heaviest things I had to carry. A sack of grain or potatoes was easy in comparison. We had to lay them on and space them with sticks so they would lie evenly. Later, we used some of the trees for building, some for wagon shafts and wheels (which would break frequently), and the worst for firewood. All summer, whenever we had spare time, we would saw and split piles of firewood for the winter, using a hand saw and an ax, just as previous generations had done. There was no sawmill nearby. We arranged the wood in long, neat rows, stacked high for drying. Skilled artisans in the village used it to build almost every necessity of daily life: water buckets, watering and feeding troughs for the cattle, garden and field tools, washtubs, dishes, platters, spoons, and so on.

After a while I got to know very well the two boys who shared my room, Jan and Tolek Jankowski, the nephews of the administrator. Their mother, the administrator's sister-in-law, moved to the farm with her young daughter after she couldn't survive in the city without work. Their father, they told me, was a high-ranking officer in the Polish army who had served as a reservist at the start of the Polish-Russian war. He was arrested by the Russians and later murdered in Katyń, along with many other officers. Naturally, they hated the Russians as well as the Germans. Their father also had been well known in Wilno as an active anti-Semite. The boys were very proud of it. I realized that in their company I had to watch every word I said and everything I did, to be alert all the time without showing it.

I also had to be careful not to physically expose myself. During that time, only Jewish men were circumcised according to the ancient religious law — not Catholics or others. When the Germans had any reason to suspect someone of being Jewish they ordered his pants down. If confirmed, it was a death sentence on the spot.

When urinating in the field I always turned away from the others, claiming shyness. Many bathed in the pond, in the nude, of course, because bathing suits were not available. I pretended to be a clean city boy who wouldn't bathe in a dirty pond full of algae and debris. Usually on Saturday afternoon and evening the farmers cleaned up for Sunday in a communal spa — a shack containing a pile of rocks under which a wood fire was built to heat them. Buckets of water were thrown on the stones, making steam. All the men went there, except for me. I used the excuse of being afraid of catching their lice. While washing or bathing in a wooden wash tub at home, I always had to be careful to avoid being seen undressed.

I also had a difficult time in my private life. I had to watch my relations with the young women in the village to avoid getting intimately involved. In their eyes, I was a polished city boy, so I was very much in demand. Although most of them were very religious they were also very promiscuous. They could not understand why I did not want any closer relationships, for, if I had wanted, any of them might have been available. There were many opportunities in the barns, on the haystacks, or in the fields. The temptation was strong, but my temperance had to be stronger. When asked why a strong, healthy young man would not want to get involved with the country girls, I generally answered, on religious grounds, that I did not want them to have to go to confession because of me, nor did I want to sin. In addition to that, some friends, acquaintances, and family members of the administrator and his wife used to come from the city to live for some time as their guests. My boss was not pleased that I didn't care for closer relations with some of the women, and had become such a snob. When asked why, I had to use all sorts of naive explanations. I absolutely couldn't get involved; it was too dangerous.

Most of the young people in the village would confess to the curate priest in the church, while the senior priest was more popular with the older folks. I could not believe it when, in our private conversations, the curate priest told me details from confessions. I had always understood that confession was supposed to be a most intimate, religious process, so I felt quite uneasy at what he was telling me and let him know how I felt. Nonetheless, he insisted on treating me as a confidante. Also, while according to his vows he was supposed to live celibately, I learned from the village physician that he didn't. The physician was the only medical doctor in the whole area. He and his wife, a pleasant and cultured couple, provided every sort of medical care—including abortions, which I learned were a big part of his practice. I was shocked when he told me about the relations between the curate priest and some local women.

Soon, there were rumors in the village that the Germans were going to select some local men to serve them in various capacities. First, however, they would conduct some sort of selective service medical examination. Only afterwards could a man be excused from serving. I knew, of course, that I would be excused from any work unit because of my document. Nevertheless, the idea of having to parade nude in front of a German scared me to death. I felt that it would be the end of me but did not see any way out. I thought about escaping but could not think where to go. I decided that whatever happened would be final.

I did have an idea, however. I had heard that there were some medical conditions, such as infection, that required a male to be circumcised for health reasons. Not really believing such a story might help me—in German eyes, no excuse existed—I nonetheless developed an urge to investigate. I had no one with whom I could discuss the matter, but I remembered having seen some old medical books in the doctor's house, piled up on a top shelf in a corner. I visited him and told him that I would like to borrow one of his books to read on Sundays. During the week there was no time to sit down and have time to oneself. Even on Sundays, there were animals to watch in the pasture and lead to water, fresh straw to be laid in the barns, feed to be prepared, cows to be milked. There were also water and wood to be brought to the house and sometimes hay and corn to be taken into the barn before a rain. Finally, whenever the boss and his wife wanted to travel, the wagon had to be prepared and the horses harnessed to it.

But the doctor was glad that someone might want to use his books. I climbed a wooden stool and reached for the first book. After I brushed away the dust and could read the titles, I found a New Testament, other religious books, and the medical books which interested me. I looked for one that dealt with male organs. At home, I studied the chapter on penis diseases. I never realized that it could be the source of so many illnesses and problems. Finally, I found what I was looking for: in acute cases of certain infections a radical circumcision was to be performed. I concocted a story of how, when I was very young, I had developed an illness and had to have an operation. I repeated it to myself many times, including the name of the hospital and the surgeon, how long I was in the hospital, and in what pain I had been. I knew that the hospital no longer existed and that the surgeon had died. I told myself the story so many times that I could repeat it perfectly if I awakened in the middle of the night. I began to believe it myself.

Looking back, I realize how naive I was to think that this story might save me. At the time I thought it was quite ingenious, and, besides, I was not able to come up with anything better. It gave me some courage, but deep inside I felt that eventually the truth would come out, that it would be my end. I played the role of a fearless hero, never letting my face show what I felt, but fear was in me every waking minute. It gave me an understanding of how a hunted animal feels. But while the animal senses danger, I don't think it realizes it may die—I did.

CHAPTER FOUR

Farmers were circulating rumors about the liquidation of Jews by the thousands in both Vilnius ghettos. They got their information when they took their products to be sold on the black market in Vilnius. I did not believe them. In my experience, farmers liked to exaggerate everything and, besides, news like that could not be real. I knew that the authorities, either German or Lithuanian, solicited bribes with the promise that the payer would be protected and not arrested; and that once the officials had everything they wanted, or everything the unfortunate victim possessed, they arrested him anyway and had his entire family killed so the truth would not be revealed. But I felt the murdering could not be happening to the extent the farmers reported. After the war, I verified that the rumors they spread were true; unfortunately, they only touched upon what actually had happened.

At the time of the German invasion, in June of 1941, the Jewish population of Vilnius was around seventy thousand. After only a few months, various "actions," as they were referred to, cut that number in half. This has been verified by official German documents discovered after the war and now archived. Mass liquidations were performed in the Ponary forest, execution-style, by Lithuanian units under the supervision of the German *Einsatzgruppen*.

Good Morning

At first, organized groups of Lithuanians and Poles, wearing white armbands, helped hunt Jews on the streets and in their homes. Each day Jewish men were arrested, and most did not return. This caused a great panic among their families and friends. They were murdered in the jails or in the Ponary Forest. The ones taken to the forest were forced to dig huge, deep pits. They were made to stand in small groups in a single line at the edge, were shot, and their bodies fell in. The next group covered the bodies with a thin layer of dirt, then were made to stand at the edge to meet the same fate. Layer by layer the pits were filled. Some escaped by cover of night and told of the horror. Witnesses said that some who were shot had not been killed, just injured as they fell in the pits with the others. They could see the thin layers of dirt on top of moving bodies.

The seventy thousand Jews of Vilnius had represented about forty percent of the city's total population. Another thirty percent or so were Lithuanian, and the remaining thirty percent were mostly Poles. Most of the non-Jews were Catholic. Most of the Catholic clergy were Polish and had lived in Vilnius from the time (before September, 1939) the city was part of Poland.

I learned that not many Jews had been able to escape before the German invasion. The army's advance had been faster than their ability to flee toward Russia. Once they found themselves under German control, those who had not been killed made their way back to Vilnius. Right from the beginning in Vilnius, while I was still residing in the city, thousands of arrested Jews had been killed by the Lithuanians. The German *Einsatzgruppen* (mobile killing squads) had not yet even had the opportunity to organize their systematic slaughter.

As I worked I was absorbed by the idea of obtaining weapons supposedly stocked by area farmers. The two Jankowski brothers with whom I lived and worked, Jan and Tolek, became very attached to me. When I felt they were mature enough to be trusted and that they might become an asset to the Underground, I had, one evening, a long, sincere talk with them. Their enthusiasm caused me to induct them the same way I had been. When I made it clear that there was no way they could back out and that some act of good faith was needed, they became impatient for any kind of action. They were popular and on good terms with the farmers in the village, so I thought they could learn through casual conversation and without creating suspicion who had stocked weapons. On the other hand, we couldn't obtain them without being recognized. The only solution was to operate in a distant area where we were not known.

This book's cover photograph of Jan, Tolek, and me was taken by a German officer. He was one of those who used to "visit" our farm. He asked us to stand in front of our "quarters," a wooden shack with a straw roof, and smile. As we were not in the mood to pose or smile, it took a command from him to get that expression. I did not believe he ever intended to give us a print, but one day some time later he arrived, happily announcing that he had something for me. I had never received anything from him, so I could not guess what it might be — perhaps some German propaganda book. To my surprise, he handed me that photograph. I guarded it for years.

On the farm, Jan and Tolek made many inquiries and learned of places where farmers were rumored to have hidden weapons. What sorts and which farmers we didn't know. Nor did we have the slightest idea who to approach in the nearby village. Late one moonlit evening we sneaked out. Our faces were smeared with ashes and our caps worn low to make us unrecognizable. I took our only revolver and a flashlight. The others took a sack in hope of loot, and we set out on foot. When we reached the outskirts of the village it was already after midnight, so we decided to stop at the first hut. I knocked loudly on the door. A sleepy voice finally answered, "Who is it?" I answered in German, "*Deutshe Polizei.*" There weren't any German police in the area, only the Lithuanian militia, but everyone was afraid of anything German. My words worked like magic. The farmer's scared face froze when I shined the flashlight in his eyes so he couldn't see us. I did not let him light a kerosene lamp, telling him that there was enough light from the full moon. He had been awakened from a deep sleep after a long day of hard work and was dazed and shaking all over. I tried to calm him, reassuring him that we were not Germans but his friends. That did not help because the farmers were afraid of any authorities. So I came right to the point: we knew that he had hidden things that in our hands might help us to defend him. He swore to God that he did not know anything and never had hidden any weapons. I did not want the discussion to drag on, so at that point I pretended to become angry.

I told him that by swearing to God and lying he was a sinner and couldn't be trusted. He would be shot if he did not get us what we wanted. I took out the revolver and aimed it at him. He got down on his knees and, crossing his heart and crying, tried to convince me that he was not hiding anything and was telling the truth. He sounded so convincing that I was ready to leave when my aide-de-camp Tolek shouted, "Kill him! He is lying!" I handed him my gun and ordered the farmer to stand in the corner and say his last prayer. I would count to three and, if he had not given us everything he had collected at that point, would have him shot. In the meantime, his wife had come into the room and, seeing strangers with blackened faces and her husband begging on his knees, began to wail. Tolek explained to her that her husband did not want to cooperate with us and therefore had to be shot. She cried to her husband asking why he wouldn't give us what we wanted. He remained in the corner, trembling and praying.

Once more, I demanded that he give us what he had. I gave the order, "Aim!" and, in the darkness of the room, we could see Tolek lift the gun and aim it at him. However, Tolek knew how far he should go — besides, the gun was not even cocked; he had never fired a revolver in his life. I counted slowly: "One . . . two . . . " Finally, the farmer said that he would give us what he had. I warned him to give us everything, because I would not be counting any more.

He led us outside to a corner of a small barn, took out a shovel, and started digging. Finally, he found the treasure wrapped in old rags and pieces of sacks. He unwrapped rusted gears and metal parts that must have come from some army vehicle. On the bottom was a single rifle, in such poor condition that I wondered if we should even bother taking it. His wife assured us that that was all they had hidden. I threw the rifle in our sack and warned him that nobody had better learn about our visit and what had happened. We had our ways to know what was being talked about in his village and, if there was even a hint that the slightest detail had gotten out, he would see his barn burn to the ground. That was a serious threat because a farmer's barn was his greatest possession, containing all the fruits of his labor.

When we returned to our farm, dawn had started to break. Daylight was an enemy, exposing us to the chance of discovery. The short summer nights meant that we always had to act quickly. We hid our sack in one side of a potato cellar, quickly washed off our "make-up," and lay down as if nothing had happened. We had to be careful that nobody noticed us, because activity on the farm started at sunrise.

The first one up was usually the farm girl who milked the cows. After that the cowherd led the cattle to the drinking trough and the pasture, keeping them from wandering away. I enjoyed the task when it was my turn and developed a good rapport with the cows. It is a common belief that cows are stupid animals, because of the expressions on their faces; it is one I do not share. I called each one by a different name, after its appearance: Blonde, Black, Brown, Spot, Whitenose, and so on. Though some were the same color, each one always had some distinguishing characteristic—like people. (Today, however, one usually sees herds in which all are the same breed and color.) The cows became so used to their names that when I called one, it would run toward me, knowing that I would give her some treat: a wormy apple, a crooked carrot, or any piece of a vegetable that I could find. It worked as well as a candy bar for a child. I didn't need to use the wooden stick that symbolized power. They did not like to be hit on the bones, which must have hurt them very much. If one wandered away into the pasture, I didn't have to run after her with the stick. I only had to call out her name, and she knew what I meant. If not, she knew that I would catch up with her and give her a good licking.

I had an unusual experience when once, as customary, I urinated on the field. The cows started running toward me. I started to run away, but the cows congregated in the place where I had stood and grazed the grass down to the bare soil. I learned later that they loved the salted grass. Before the war, when salt was readily available and inexpensive, blocks of it were placed in the pasture for the cows to lick. This would make them drink more water which, in turn, was supposed to make them produce more milk. The incident taught me that when urinating in the fields I had to be wary, not only of people, but also of cows. I tried to hide behind bushes if some were near. Even though the cows never seemed to look at me, being absorbed in their grazing, they still managed to notice whenever I headed toward the bushes. Like pigs, the cows would drink any water they found. In contrast, horses would drink only perfectly clean water. If there was a blade of grass floating in their water they wouldn't drink it.

I learned quite a bit about different animals, farming, fish raising, and fighting during those four years. I also learned a lot about Germans. I was given a German military manual, one that had been issued by the Wehrmacht, valuable to me for the insights into a German soldier's behavior, tactics, and so on. The best way to defeat an enemy is to know him well.

To build up our inventory of weapons, we made frequent "visits" to farmers, always performing the same script. Each time they would swear not to have anything. Each time we would have to pretend to be merciless. There wasn't a time we came away empty-handed. Though I always tried to assuage their feelings before we left. I felt they hated us for what we had done to them. Our biggest job was to clean up everything we had accumulated. We did it a piece at a time, after everyone else was asleep. It was also difficult to find a safe and dry place in which to hide the weapons.

The Lithuanian militia soon started snooping around in our area during the night as they already had during the day. Our activities became increasingly dangerous. They were looking for anything out of the ordinary, especially for Jews who had fled the ghettos and hidden, seeking ways to escape east. One dawn, as we were leaving for work, some drunken militiamen came to see who was living on the farm. They wandered from room to room. When they came to ours, they asked how many people lived in it. When I answered, three, they accused me of lying because they knew there were more people. They demanded to know where the others were hiding. I showed them the *Bescheinigung* (document) that I had received earlier and told them that I was employed by the German authorities and felt offended that they were calling me a liar. They knew I was showing them some kind of German document, but they couldn't read it. Being drunk, they insisted that there must be more people because there were eight hats hanging on hooks. When I laughingly explained that some were winter caps and two were the boys' Sunday hats, they left unhappily. No one was supposed to laugh at the militia; everyone was supposed to be afraid of them. In truth, I was afraid, more than anyone around, but I forced myself not to show it.

During one of our nightly escapades a small, chained-up dog started barking at us. This started other dogs barking and, soon, it sounded as if all the dogs of the village were barking. This was dangerous, for soon the farmers would realize there were either wolves or strangers approaching. As I neared the dog he barked even more ferociously. I pointed my flashlight at him so he couldn't see me, but I could see his bared teeth and staring eyes. He growled and snarled at me, so I took out my revolver, approached still closer, and aimed between his eyes. He was moving around so much I wasn't sure I could hit him. When he froze for a moment, I pulled the trigger, the first time I had fired my gun. The noise and its echo were terrible. He fell instantly, and we ran as fast as we could to the woods, our best protection.

I knew that I had done the wrong thing. By shooting I had alerted all the villagers that something was wrong. But drunken militiamen often shot at something suspicious (anything that moved during the night was suspicious) or just for fun to scare the people. And the barking of the dogs could have exposed us. Still the picture of that snarling dog left me with an unpleasant feeling. I had killed a small, innocent animal trying to protect its master. On the other hand, I was encouraged that the revolver was working properly and that I could depend on it if I had to.

Some time later I received an order to disrupt a communications line, a telephone line for the exclusive use of the Luftwaffe that supposedly ran directly from the Eastern front to Berlin. We called it the "air line." We equipped ourselves with two sharp wood saws, traveled a few kilometers down the road, and quickly toppled two wooden telephone poles. We had to act fast because German traffic frequently passed down this main road. Happily, we returned home feeling our task was well accomplished. The following day, though, was a sad one. We learned that the line had been repaired almost immediately. Worse yet, a few innocent young people from the area closest to the damage were taken by the authorities and never returned home.

We realized that we would have to operate in areas where no one lived. This was a problem, as we had no transportation suitable for distances. Motor vehicles were out of the question (they were noisy and unavailable anyway), and we didn't have bicycles. We had to move quietly, using paths, fields, ditches, and trenches that a vehicle couldn't negotiate. The only alternative was horses, which could travel on any terrain. But the farm horses worked hard during the day. We needed them at night, when they rested and fed in the stables or grazed in the fields, so we had to act like horse thieves.

Horses could negotiate forests, too. We learned that the woods were the safest areas. The Germans did not like them and considered each tree an enemy. They could not tell who might be hiding on or behind one. Only the bigger and better-equipped units dared to enter the forests. It was well known that the partisan groups formed by the remnants of the Russian Army, the People's Army (Armia Ludowa), and units of the National Army (Armia Krajowa), as well as some families and individuals in hiding, found the safest haven in the woods.

Our next mission, again to interrupt communications by severing the "air line," was more sophisticated. I picked up some special connectors in town. I was told to secure the connector/insulator to the wire, as close as I could to the wooden post, and then to loop it around. The other end would then be attached as close as possible to the same live wire. After assuring that the connector was well-secured on both ends, we were to cut the live wire between. Neither the cable nor the pole would show signs of tampering. My fireman's training came in handy when I climbed the poles. We repeated this process on several occasions in various locations. While the Germans were efficient at repairing the damage, the interruptions were thought to be important.

In a further effort to thwart these disruptions, the Germans built a special cable buried underground. Then I was instructed to haul containers of acid from town. We dug holes where the cable was buried and poured acid in them, filling them in afterwards so that nothing would look disturbed. It took some time since the acid had to penetrate the cable. These efforts gave the Germans problems, too. I was eventually told that they finally turned to overhead lines and coded radio transmissions. But since I never received any more orders involving the communications lines I did not know what was happening—whether the sabotage had been abandoned, had become someone else's responsibility, or the activities had moved to some other territory. I did not ask, then. The less I knew, the safer it was.

Whenever some contraband had to be brought from Vilnius, I volunteered to deliver vegetables or whatever needed to be sent from the farm. I would have official papers requesting the delivery. This also gave me the use of a good horse or two horses and the big wagon filled with plenty of straw. Anything that needed to come back could be wrapped in straw and used as a seat, covered with dirty old blankets.

I received word that we would be working to slow down the convoys passing on the highway. I was to pick up a load of boxes of nails. On a particular night we would spread some in various spots along the road, where they would puncture the tires of the passing vehicles. Other groups would be doing the same further down the road. The military traffic made the task dangerous, because if we were caught it would be a disaster for us. But we got results. A convoy had to stop and replace their tires with spares. When they ran out of spares they had to repair the tires, which took even longer.

Later, rollers with magnetic brushes were installed on the fronts of the transport trucks, making our nails almost useless. In turn, special aluminum spikes were developed. They did not look like regular nails, but like a distorted, squashed Z, with sharp points on both ends. When they were ready, I picked up the spikes from town, but had a close call. I had hidden them in a big wagon piled high with straw. As I turned off from the main to the side road leading to the farm, I made a sharp turn to the right. One wheel dropped into the ditch, causing the wagon to tilt and spilling all the straw that covered the boxes. I immediately jumped from the wagon and threw straw onto the boxes to cover them. I supported the right rear corner of the wagon with my shoulder and ordered the horse to move. The wagon straightened more easily than I had expected, so then I quickly reloaded the spilled straw with my hands. As I was doing this a small army pickup truck stopped and a soldier approached. Not knowing his intentions I continued to load the straw with my bare hands, not changing my tempo. I pretended not to see him, being absorbed with my work. When he reached me he asked if he could help. It was unusual for a farmhand in this area to speak German. Russian and Polish were more likely. Not realizing that I understood him he also pantomimed his offer. I politely thanked him but suggested that he had more important things to do than to help me. He was surprised that I answered him in German and asked how I knew the language, to which I replied I had learned it in Vilnius. He saw that I was absorbed with my task and not eager to get into a conversation with him, so he said good-bye.

My encounters with German soldiers had led me to expect that one who approached a civilian politely, especially a farmer, was trying to gain something. I imagine this one thought I was carrying fresh dairy products, like eggs or butter, and that he might be able to get some. As fast as I could, I drove home with my cargo, where the boys, already expecting me, helped me to unload it in the barn. We would have easy access to it there. The boxes of aluminum nails were light compared to the iron ones. I could not stop berating myself for my carelessness, though.

On the main roads leading to Vilnius were sentries who checked every wagon and its contents entering or leaving the city. If a wagon looked suspicious or was piled high with straw or hay they would poke it with their bayonets, looking for something or someone hidden within. This was the reason I never traveled without a document requesting delivery of produce from our farm. As a sentry approached and began to ask questions I showed him the document and explained, in German, that this was a request for delivery from our farm, which was under German administration. They seldom asked any more questions, though sometimes they wanted to know who I was and to see my personal documents.

One experience increased my anger and hatred toward the Germans. The farm received a request for a wagonload of hay to be delivered to the Jewish ghetto in Vilnius. Wagons were the only transportation there. Most were pulled by people, but some, for official use, were pulled by horses. The hay was supposed to be used as horse feed. No one on the farm wanted to deliver it. They claimed to be afraid of catching some disease from the filthy Jews and considered the ghetto an island of pestilence. I played the role of the fearless hero and volunteered for the job. I simply wanted to know what was going on inside the ghetto. I had heard so many gruesome stories. I also wanted to erase any possible suspicion that I might be a Jew. After all, Jews were trying to escape from the ghetto, not trying to get in. After I volunteered I realized how stupid I had been. If by chance anybody recognized me there, I would be lost. But the chance to see for myself if the situation was as hopeless as people had been relating calmed my fears. But I was fully aware that I was putting my head in the lion's mouth. I always did have a tendency toward embarking upon dangerous ventures.

The day before I was to leave, the sleigh was loaded high with hay. It was secured with a rope so the load wouldn't shift or fall on the uneven roads. Very early the following morning I harnessed the horse by the light of a kerosene lamp and drove off. I made sure to have all the documents I would need, plus extras. It was dark and very windy, and it felt very, very cold. Falling snow blew into every gap in my clothing. For this trip I was loaned high woolen boots, very popular in Russia, called *woywoki* (pronounced more like "voywoki" in English), and a long bulky fur coat, made from sheepskins, which had a hood and a huge collar to keep my face from freezing. This was the only fur coat on the farm and was reserved for use during these long winter trips. I was glad that my face was completely covered, except for a small opening for my eyes. I convinced myself that no one could recognize me. Along with this attire I sported a large, thick mustache, making me look like a typical peasant farmer. After a short time white frost from my breath accumulated around the opening of the coat. (On cold days when I was not wearing the fur coat frost around my mustache turned into ice that I could break off.)

The ride was very quiet. I could hear only the sleigh squeaking and crackling as it broke the frozen surface of the snow, especially on the side roads. I assured myself that the small sack containing my food was securely tied to a bar inside the sleigh. I wouldn't be able to get anything to eat in town, so I would be without food all day if it was lost or stolen. I had two half slices of farmers bread with a thin layer of lard spread between. The lard was a luxury, which I got because of the trip. I also had a small tin container with some moonshine to keep me warm. I hated moonshine, but I considered it a necessary medicine. Finally, I got a round loaf of farmers bread that I was supposed to sell in the ghetto for a high price. I was surprised that my boss let me take it, as smuggling food into the ghetto was a capital offense. But I couldn't refuse. I suggested that it be cut into quarters so that it would sell more easily.

It is hard to understand today what a treasure a big, round loaf of farmers bread was. It meant life or death in the ghetto. Even in town bread hardly tasted right or had the proper consistency. It was rumored to contain a large amount of fine sawdust. Like other essentials, if they were available at all, bread was sold only for ration coupons that were distributed monthly.

The journey was uneventful. At the outskirts of town my cargo, by then dusted with snow, was given only a cursory look. I assume that was because at the moment I was stopped I immediately handed over the requisition for the delivery. Besides, it was so cold that the sentry wanted to get out of the open. When I reached the ghetto, it was another story. It was already daylight, and I was stopped at the gate. The Germans were assisted by Lithuanians, who wore different uniforms. When I handed them my papers they conversed among themselves. One German soldier went inside to make a phone call. After a while they asked if I had anything else besides hay. Instead of answering I asked why I should bring anything else if I had an order to bring the damned hay from such a distance. They told me where to unload the hay and to leave immediately afterwards.

When I drove in, the scene was indescribable and haunts me to this day. I had planned to ask many questions and to make many inquiries; but once I entered, my mind went blank. I froze completely. I did not see people but miserable ghosts dressed in rags. The entire time I was in the ghetto I saw no one smiling, which would have been out of the question, and not even one relaxed face. Most of them must have known their fate, but surely there must have been some spark of hope in them. If there was, however, I could not detect it. I imagine that criminals on death row must feel better than any of those people did. No photograph could express the emotions I felt from them. A painting would show them as fearful ghosts. I must have been their dream, a well-fed, stern-looking character without any human feelings, a simple farmer, dressed warmly and free to do what he pleased.

It was very cold. I expected that the Jews would be walking briskly to warm themselves but I saw figures dragging their feet. There was a heavy wagon being pulled along by two people harnessed to it. I untied my bundle containing the bread and unobtrusively "lost" it along with my half-sandwich. I drove on as if nothing had happened. Suddenly, from the edge of my vision I noticed a commotion and people following me. I raised the horsewhip and

yelled, pretending that I wanted to hit them. I had to repeat the scene a few times until they went away.

As soon as the hay was unloaded, I drove as fast as I
could from that hell. The fear and horror of what I had
seen left me in a daze. At the gate on the way out the
guards checked to see if anybody was hiding under the
sleigh trying to escape. The sleigh was so low that I could
not understand how anyone might hang under it.

When I reached the highway I was hungry, but the
thought of eating my now-frozen slice of bread made me
nauseous. I felt remorseful and selfish for having not "lost"
it, too. I took nips of the moonshine I had been given for
the road from a small container, holding perhaps two
shots. I hated the stuff though, having drunk a lot of it
while it was being made in the village. I didn't have to
use the horsewhip at all; the horse was heading home at a
very good pace. Without the load, the sleigh glided
smoothly. But I returned home very upset. I publicly attributed it to having had my bread stolen from me. I told
them that while the hay was being unloaded I fed the horse
and went to the latrine. I had kept the bread unpacked
because I had wanted to sell it. When I returned after a
moment the bread was gone. I hadn't been able to do anything about it because I was afraid of being caught smuggling illegal goods into the ghetto.

I thought it was a good excuse, but I didn't know
whether I was really believed. I wondered if they thought
I had sold the bread and kept the money for myself. I later
learned from the boys, the nephews of my boss, that my
story had been believed. They also knew that I didn't have
any money. Nonetheless, I insisted that some day I would
pay for the damage, and I did. When I was paid a basket
of grain from the farmer for occasionally teaching German to his children, I gave it to the manager.

Good Morning

Each farmer had to get a permit in order to use a certain portion of his crops and other commodities, such as seeds and cattle feed. The rest had to be delivered to a staging area. I did not know of any farmer who reported the size of his crop honestly. Though the Lithuanian authorities were very helpful in reporting to the Germans any discrepancies from the estimates they had made, it was hard for them to enforce the rule. Nevertheless, almost every farmer had some "surplus" crops and livestock. These were his only currency. To purchase a horse or cow, to hire a farmhand, to pay for a stallion to fecundate his mares, no money was exchanged, only a certain quantity of grain or other produce.

Since no whiskey was available, the farmers had to make it themselves, though this was also strictly forbidden by the Germans. I hated the local moonshine and even now can't stand Scotch whisky because its smell reminds me of it. The moonshine was distilled from ground rye grain, the same used for making bread. They called their moonshine *samogonek*. The name seems appropriate, because it was produced during the night in the woods by the light of the moon. The mash had to be prepared in advance so that it would start to ferment. This was also done in the woods, not at home, because its strong odor could give it away to officials in the vicinity.

On a designated day at an agreed upon location, deep in the woods, a few farmers would gather for a feast. A primitively made still was brought, as was a "spare" young pig for slaughter. After being invited to my first of these events there wasn't one to which I wasn't honored by being asked. I would rather have been absent, though, because having them was dangerous, and I didn't need to take any more risks. Also, I hated them.

The first time, I was honored with the task of killing the small pig. I begged off, assuring them I would ruin the event because I had never killed a pig or even seen how it was done. They tried to persuade me that there was nothing to it: I was bigger than the pig; they would hold it and point out the heart for me to pierce with a sharp knife. The thought made me sick. When I insisted that I could not do it, they bestowed upon me another honor: to collect the blood from the wound in a wide bowl. From this blood and groats was made a sausage called "czarnina," very prized and considered a rarity. I couldn't talk myself out of that one.

The stabbed pig was squealing loudly. It seemed as if the entire forest would be awakened. Blood poured from the wound as if from a fountain. I didn't know what I was doing and was so frightened that they had to maneuver my hands. When the full pan was taken from me I sighed with relief. By this time the first liquid had started trickling out of the still. The first was considered the best, having the highest alcohol concentration. While the farmers tasted it they needed a snack, so they cut off pieces of the pig's ears and roasted them over the fire. When the ears were gone the owner gutted the pig, cutting a piece of belly and roasting it. When it was ready he gave everyone some of the bacon. The alternation of tasting the running moonshine and snacking on the pig continued until an expert declared the brew too weak to collect. The mash was poured into a small barrel that was loaded onto a wagon for the owner to take home. He mixed it with straw chaff and fed it to the cattle. It was supposed to be very healthy for them. I found out later that it at least made them happy—happily tipsy.

One morning on the farm we heard the two chained

dogs barking viciously. This was an indication that a strange person or animal was approaching, or was already on, the farm. At their signal, everyone who was inside immediately ran out to see what was going on. We spotted two German officers with hunting guns walking by one of the ponds. The administrator, standing nearby, winked at me to investigate. I walked toward the Germans, slowly, so as not to show any anxiety or excitement. When I approached them in my shabby clothing, they looked at me suspiciously with arrogant smiles. But when I greeted them with a "Good morning," in German, and politely asked if they were looking for something or if I could be of any help, their faces immediately changed. They were surprised at my perfect German. They knew about our farm and fish hatcheries, but asked me what I was doing there. They wanted to know if I was a *Volksdeutsche* (of German extraction) that I spoke German so well.

I explained everything to them, keeping to the truth, as was my policy, whenever it was possible and safe. That way I did not have to remember what lies I had told, should I have to repeat the same story. I told them that I was not a *Volksdeutsche.* Only my mother, whose maiden name was Grün, was German. My father was Polish. I knew German because I had learned it in school and later studied in Vienna. I had graduated during the period when Austria was under the Nazi protectorate. I also told them how proud I was that my diploma bore a seal with a swastika. (I told them this last because I realized from their German accents that they were not Austrians, many of whom served in the German army.) I said that the territory from which I came had been annexed and was now considered a part of the liberated German state. Nonetheless, I planned to return there as soon as the war was over, as I had been born there and considered it my home. They insisted that I was a *Volksdeutsche,* but I said I wished that I was so I wouldn't have to work as hard.

The Germans said they had come with their hunting guns to shoot some of the wild ducks they had seen in the vicinity. I suggested that the best time might be early in the morning when we sometimes had to chase geese away with stones so that they would not eat our small fish. We had more conversation, and I asked them if they would be willing to go inside the building. As we approached the group, which wondered what was going on, I explained to the administrator the purpose of their visit. I introduced them to him and asked him, to the side, if he wanted to treat them with some refreshments. He immediately understood what I meant and ordered the farm maid to prepare fried eggs with bacon and dark farm bread with a small piece of butter. He personally brought in a bottle of moonshine. When I described the treat Tadeusz had for them, the officers' eyes glittered as if they had struck gold. They ate everything, cleaning the wooden plates with their bread so that it was almost unnecessary to wash them. It was not that they were hungry—their round faces belied that—but this kind of fresh food was prized by Germans who were away from the military centers. They did not drink the moonshine, saying that they had good schnapps in their quarters and would bring some next time. They wanted to buy butter and lard to send to their families in Germany. They even offered to barter some whiskey or another article we might need. We did need many items for ourselves and for the farm. Even salt was short, not to mention such luxuries as sugar. Of course, they would give us those articles by confiscating them from others or by pilfering their army supplies. I immediately explained that the administrator would be willing to give some to them, but these foods were in great shortage for us. We did not get a treat as they did every day, but only on special holidays. What they had eaten came out of the rations of all of us who worked on the farm.

I thought that they would apologize and feel some kind of remorse, but I judged wrongly. They were not fazed. I continued by explaining that we were ordered to deliver all the crops, including fish, to the depot and were allowed to keep only a small amount for our rations as approved by the administration. They indicated that they were acquainted with the arrangements, but they knew that every farmer in the village tried to cheat. That was why the Lithuanians were keeping such a tight grip. I pretended to feel offended by their remark, saying that we had been informed that our products were being supplied to the army. We had even received a letter from the administration to that effect. I do not know if this made any impression on them.

Of course the Lithuanians collaborated with the Nazis. In our area, especially, the Lithuanian militia blackmailed and terrorized the poor farmers to the extent that they did not have enough to feed their own families and livestock. They used various pretexts to confiscate grain and flour for distilling moonshine in large quantities. They did the same with other staples which farmers had worked hard to accumulate for the rough winters. It was generally known that at the depot run by Lithuanians, where everyone who had milk cows was supposed to send a certain amount of their whole milk, all kinds of fraud and deceit were occurring. The Lithuanians skimmed the milk of its fat, then accused the farmers of doing so. Under threat, the farmers had to bribe them and privately give them all kinds of farm goods. At first, with all the gossip we heard, we did not believe these stories. Then it happened to us.

One day, the worker who delivered milk from our farm (Tolek, my right-hand man in all my military endeavors) returned upset. He said that they had ordered him to warn "the people on the hill" (as some people called us, because the farm was located on the higher land in the area) not to skim the milk as others were doing. The administrator asked me to go and straighten out the situation. We agreed on the message I should carry. At the depot I repeated what the worker had said, telling them that they had made a very grave accusation. Because the farm was officially under German administration we were obliged to officially report any improprieties to the office in Vilnius. I asked them for a written statement so we could enclose it with our report to the authorities. I told the clerk that although I knew he was a trustworthy, good, hard-working boy and the nephew of the administrator, he nevertheless would have to be investigated. We knew that the milk was leaving the farm in the proper condition because we had a special instrument to test it (that was a lie). The authorities had given it to us for this purpose to see whether the cows were in good health and properly fed. As I said this, I was feeling very frightened and tense, though I did not show it outwardly. I felt more secure after seeing the fear on their faces. This helped my courage. I became bolder in our conversation, aggressively demanding "the necessary document for the authorities." I dropped the matter when one man contritely offered to forget the incident, suggesting it may have been an isolated case or a situation where they had inadvertently exchanged our milk with someone else's. I was fortunate that the situation ended this way, as it could have been a disaster for me. Whether they were drunk or sober, one did not know what might happen when dealing with the Lithuanians.

Later, I had even more reason to be grateful after I learned why the wife of the farm administrator handled all the milk herself. After the cows were milked, usually very early in the morning and in the evening when they returned from the pasture, all the milk was delivered to her. She supposedly had to filter out any debris and measure out the ration used by the humans and cattle on the farm. (All calves were taken away from their mothers shortly after birth and fed by hand. The milk was diluted with water and mixed with some flour. A maid would immerse her hand in this drink and gave a finger to the calf to suck until it learned to drink by itself. Some milk was also used as a supplement for newborn piglets when the sow had too many to feed herself.) The administrator's wife then lowered the milk container into the water well, where it was always cool in the summer and supposedly for better preservation. Once the milk was cool, though, the cream rose to the top and she skimmed it off for herself and her husband. This was also the reason they always had butter.

Early in the morning of the following day, the German officers returned to hunt, bringing an extra hunting gun for me. I refused, explaining that I did not know how to handle it and that I might get hurt or cause some kind of accident. They tried to explain that there was nothing to it and that they would teach me. I was greatly tempted for a moment and thought about ostentatiously displaying the shotgun on the wall of our hut. When I considered

the kind of predicament I could get myself into, I categori-
cally refused, claiming that when the Lithuanian militia
saw it they would shoot me or would arrest everyone at
the farm. The officers laughed and offered to give me some
kind of written permit, but I meekly refused, playing
dumb and frightened of weapons.

We walked around the ponds, but I could not find any
ducks that day. The two hunters left without firing a shot.
I apologized that, because of the nice weather, everyone
was very busy in the fields and "felt very sorry" that we
could not socialize. Actually, I was glad that they did not
demand anything. They left, promising to return. Their
visits became more frequent and included other officers.
The introduction was always the same: "Our friend, Josef."
Though I was only a worker, busy most of the time,
dressed in shabby clothing, and dirty from working in the
fields, the administrator asked me to take care of the
"guests." Tadeusz Zaborski did not want much to do with
them. Also, he could not communicate well with them,
and I always served as translator. One time an officer came
who could converse in good Polish. He said that he was
partially of Polish descent. I did not dare to ask where he
was from and avoided any unnecessary discussion on that
topic, feeling that the less it was brought up, the less I
might be asked. I was afraid to get into any discussion
with him, as it seemed to me that he knew too much and
that I seemed a doubtful character to him. The way he
looked at me scared me. He kept his head bowed down,
his eyes looking up suspiciously. It seemed to me that he
thought I was not the person I appeared to be. He also
looked very rough and acted with abruptness, showing
his superiority.

The officers began to invite me to their barracks. I decided their reason was that they expected me not to come empty-handed. Chicken eggs did the trick. Personally, I felt uneasy with their "friendship." One day they informed me that there was a program for leasing horses and other equipment no longer fit for army use at their headquarters in Vilnius. The farm administrator asked me to investigate and gave me a free hand to deal. The horses could be "rented" by civilian organizations which were under German or Lithuanian authority. After a period of time they had to be brought back for examination. If and when they recuperated to where they were fit for army use, they had to be exchanged for another weakling. The soldier at the stables later told me this seldom happened. Tadeusz obtained a request form from the administrative office in Vilnius. It stated that the farm was in need of horses and other equipment to be used for production on the farm premises. We were all optimistic. On the farm, they had told me how to choose a good horse: First, look at the teeth in the horse's mouth to determine its age. Then, note how it looks and is built, how it keeps its head up, walks, runs, and so on.

When I finally found, with much difficulty and dread, the army barn headquarters, they allowed me to enter the office. I presented the documents. They took them, looked at me from head to toe, asked what I was doing on the farm and, as I later learned, were surprised that I had not brought anything with me. A soldier took the documents with him, returned after a long time with other papers for me to sign and to have me pay the fee. After the transaction he called someone on the telephone, then told me to go outside and wait for the horse.

A soldier in a loose, shabby uniform approached me leading a limping horse. He asked in a harsh voice, "Farmhouse Rukojnie?" When I responded, he handed me the rope tied around the horse's neck. I asked if I could get a stronger horse for working on the farm. He answered, "This is what we have. This is what you get. Good ones we need for our own use."

I took what I got and went with him to where I had left the farm's horse and small, empty wagon. The horse neighed when he saw me approaching. I thought he was happy to see me. He was standing still and had finished his portion of hay. I put his gear and harness on in preparation for the trip back home. The horses were always happy and usually ran faster when they realized they were returning.

We always carried emergency rations for the horses. I opened a small bucket of oats to give to the new member of the family, hoping that he would rapidly devour it. But he took only a few slow mouthfuls, even though he was skin and bones. I thought that he might not be hungry, but seldom did a horse refuse such a treat. Later, while we were on our way, I gave him some water, but he was not very interested in that either. I tied him alongside the wagon so he would have no load to pull. He was very slow, and I had to slow down so he could keep up with the farm's horse. When he became very tired, I parked the wagon by the side of the road and led him to some green grass by the ditch. That did not appeal to him either. Finally, we arrived at the farm.

When the experts looked at him, I was not praised for my choice. They cleaned him up a little, gave him fresh water to drink, and prepared his supper, mashed potatoes mixed with oats. Fresh hay was hanging over his trough that he could help himself to. I wished that they would fuss as much over me and the other workers as they did the animals on the farm.

Good Morning

The bad news came the next morning. Tolek, usually the first at the horsebarn to attend them, came running to tell us that the new horse was lying down. He was lying on the clean straw that had been spread on the floor for him. A horse down was a bad sign. A horse normally sleeps or rests standing up. He might lie down for a little while in the green pastures to scratch his back, but he gets up easily on his own. This horse must have been ill. But when I received it, they handed me a receipt and a statement which I had to sign. It stated that horse number so-and-so was healthy, having been checked by the army veterinarian, and had to be returned healthy in the same or better condition, for which we were responsible. Therefore our horse "experts" on the farm felt that he had been abused and was weak. With a good rest, feed, and care, we should have a good, strong working horse.

Getting the horse to stand up was not easy, even with strong people experienced with them. I never realized how heavy a horse was. It was an awkward task, especially as we took care not to injure him. We slid a wide board under his belly, aided by the thick layer of straw underneath. We got him up, but he was unsteady on his weak legs. Soon he staggered and lay down again. This time, they decided to lift him up part way then slide a heavy canvas blanket under his belly. They tied the top edges of the blanket to a rope, threw the rope over a beam, and used the improvised sling to lift the horse to a standing position. When he was able to stand by himself they tied the rope to a lower beam so he would be supported upright. They left the horse like that for a few days, not letting him outside. He started to gain some strength. His skin looked better, and he seemed to be gaining weight. The farmhands began to take him out for some walks. Things seemed to be going fine until the morning of the tenth day, when Tolek found him dead.

I immediately set off for Vilnius to report what had happened, yet without the proper documents could not gain entrance to the place where I had originally gotten the horse. I had to return home without accomplishing anything. The road was rough and dusty. I could feel my heavy boots, whose very thick soles were made of old tires. The forty-kilometer (twenty-five mile) round trip was hard. Above all, for me to go to the city was more than an unpleasant task. I was always afraid that something might go wrong: I might be identified and never return. But I couldn't show my feelings or share them with anyone. I tried to talk myself into thinking fatalistically. I did believe that I would not live through the war. I wanted to live one month past its end to see the outcome, so I tried to develop plans (mostly unrealistic, given my capabilities and situation) to hurt the enemy. This gave me the courage and energy to act aggressively.

The second day after the horse's death Tadeusz and I went by horse and wagon to the administration facilities. I stayed with the wagon while Tadeusz went to the office to report the event and learn what to do. He returned with a long written report and a statement saying that we definitely needed a strong horse for farm work. From there we went to the army barn headquarters. This time, Tadeusz stayed with the parked wagon and sent me to get another horse. He took a nap on the straw in the wagon while I sweated, not knowing the reaction I could expect in the military office. I might be accused of killing the horse, property of the German military. They valued horses more than human beings they considered non-Aryan.

I approached a soldier who accepted the written report and the requisition very quietly, almost like a person accepting a eulogy for a friend. I told him the entire story of the last ten days of the horse's life. As I was afraid of being accused of having sold the horse, I told him that I did not know what proof I could bring, other than the report. Perhaps a piece of the horse's hide that had been branded with its number? To my surprise, he burst into laughter, saying, "It is better that the horse died on the farm than in our barn — less bother."

After reading the report and the requisition from the German Civilian Administration, he went to the phone. I did not hear what he said, but he laughed several times during the conversation. Finally, he returned to the counter and stated in a formal voice that the surplus horses had not yet been processed. I should return on a particular day, about two weeks away, to obtain one. He handed me a slip of paper, a requisition for one horse. I was thinking that perhaps it should have specified a "half-dead horse, one that was unfit even for making into glue." At the bottom was a note: "Replacement for dead horse, number. . ."

I thanked him and left. When Tadeusz saw me approach without a horse, his expression was one I had never seen on him. But I told him what had transpired, and we left for home in a hurry.

I returned on the specified day. Showing the requisition, I had no difficulty entering the area and getting another horse. The soldier who brought it to me said that, while it might look small, it would be a good one for the farm. It was strong and healthy but too small for army use. We never returned the horse, keeping it through the end of the war. I used it many times in action against the Germans. We named it Stuka, after the German airplane. (The dead horse had been called Fokker after another one.)

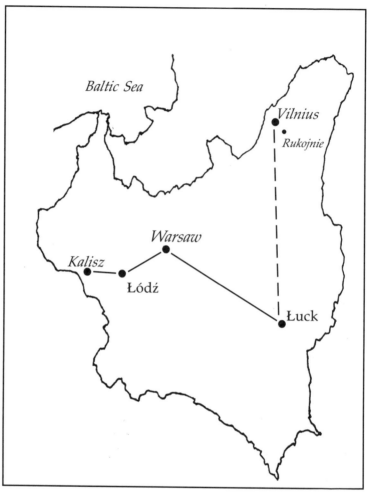

Baltic Sea

Vilnius

Rukojnie

Warsaw

Kalisz

Łódź

Łuck

This map traces Joseph Stevens's movements during the Second World War. He left Kalisz on August 31, 1939, journeying by fire truck to Łódź, and then by bicycle to Warsaw and Łuck, where he arrived on September 17th. Three months later, Stevens traveled to Vilnius by sleigh and on foot, arriving in the Lithuanian city in January of 1940. After the German conquest of Vilnius in June 1941, and the institution of anti-Jewish measures, he sought a farm job in the small village of Rukojnie, some fifteen miles to the southeast. The site of his many Resistance activities, he remained there until the arrival of the Red Army in the middle of June 1944.

Lila, Józef, and Abraham Szczecinski, 1926

Szczecinski family, c. 1936. Abraham, Lila, Józef, and Jacob (father)
Helena Grün (mother)

High School photograph, 1936. Józef is on far left

Passport photograph, 1936   *Russian identification card, 1940*

Start Pen publicity material

Left: Józef Szczecinski and Hela Lev, Vilnius, 1941

Below: German identification card, Vilnius, 1941

Bottom: Janek and Tolek Jankowski with "Szczupak," c. 1942

Breslau, 1946

JÓZEF SZCZECIŃSKI
DYREKTOR
Państwowych Zakładów Graficznych Nr. 2

WROCŁAW   MATTHIASSTR. 88

Business card, 1946

Mary Fuchs Szczecinski, 1945

Above: Joseph Stevens, 1949

Opposite top: Letterhead from National Lithograph, Detroit
Middle: Joseph Stevens, ca.1960s
Bottom: Business card, Scribner Avenue location

NATIONAL LITHOGRAPH COMPANY
OFFSET COLOR LITHOGRAPHERS

TELEPHONE
TR. 5-4665

723 EAST MILWAUKEE AVENUE
DETROIT 2, MICHIGAN

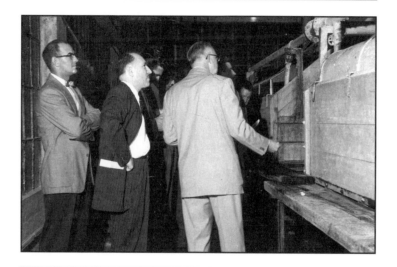

CHAPTER FIVE

❧❧

These were the experiences of my days. Those of my nights were kept from all but "our people," when we operated under the protection of darkness. During the summer, the nights were very short. Nights in the winter were long, better for our purposes, but winter was severe. Everything was covered with snow, which did not melt until late in the spring, and which made our tracks easy to follow. Fortunately for us, there were many windstorms, which obscured the tracks, as well as snowstorms, which covered them.

Most of our activities, until later in the war, were to delay, disrupt, and destroy, insofar as possible, the convoys headed for the Eastern front. They carried men, equipment, and many kinds of supplies. Trucks transporting gasoline made the easiest targets and supplied the most dramatic results. Ammunition and other explosives, on the other hand, were shipped in protective containers hard for our weapons to penetrate from a distance.

Once, an expert came to help us lay mines on the road. He brought them himself, but the results of the risky preparation did not repay the effort. We usually operated on both sides of the road, aiming toward the vehicles as they approached. That way, our crossfire created more confusion among the unprepared Germans but did not endanger ourselves. In the winter, before any action, we prepared the ground. A few of our people ran back and forth on each side of the road between the highway and the woods behind, our only safe haven. This left what looked like the tracks of many people in the snow to confuse the Germans, who usually investigated afterwards.

In fact, only a few of us took part in any action. That was all we could spare, for two reasons. First, my group was not large. Second, if we had been wiped out, the losses would have been noticeable in the village and the Germans would have made reprisals on the innocent peasants. Therefore, each of us was from a different area. We did not carry documents or anything else that could identify us. Instead, we carried some items that pointed to Vilnius, Kaunas, or some other Lithuanian or Ukrainian city. Certainly we did not wear uniforms of any kind, though occasionally someone had a Russian, German, or Polish helmet. We usually darkened our faces with a dirty cloth so if we should be spotted we would not be good targets. We avoided any direct confrontations because of German superiority in men and firepower. We would have been the losers.

I was always prepared to end it for myself if I realized that I was about to be captured, in any condition. I knew that I would not be able to withstand the Germans' torture. Once they extracted information from me that I should not have revealed, they would realize that I was of no more use to them and I would be shot anyway. For that reason I always wore shirts with two pockets, one on each side. If a shirt did not already have them, I asked one of the farm girls to sew them on for me. (I told them that I kept things in them because I was used to doing so in the city. One of the least sophisticated and educated farm girls was especially accommodating. She felt privileged to do any chore for me and washed my clothes when needed.) I used the two pockets to hold cyanide capsules: one in each. If the situation ever called for it, I could quickly reach a pocket on either side. The capsules were wrapped so they would not break accidentally, for they were supposed to break easily in the mouth. I was assured by the people who supplied four of them to me that they were very dependable. No one else knew of them other than Jan and Tolek. They also knew where the other two were hidden.

On the farm I always made sure during the summer that one of "our people" watched the horses grazing during the evening of a planned action. That way, no one else would notice us sneaking out at night. Secondly, if I needed a horse, he could have one, already harnessed and fed with an extra portion of oats and water. Finally, he would prepare any other gear we needed.

We had to return to the farm before light. If I did not make it to the farm on time, it should be taken as a sign that I would never return. My two trusted coworkers, Jan and Tolek, who were the only ones directly involved with me in the Underground, had a procedure they would follow. They would spread the word in the morning that occasionally I had been sneaking out at night to meet a mysterious girl farmhand. Perhaps I had gotten drunk and slept in some barn or ditch. Or I might have sneaked out to some moonshine party. They supposed it was in some distant village, probably in the opposite direction from the highway where the action was carried out.

Each time I quietly left the farm everything was prepared for me. Not a word was exchanged with anyone, as voices on a quiet night carried very well to the village. A dog barking, the snort of a horse, a rooster's crow, a hawk, or a wolf could be heard from far away. Our farm was on a hill, letting me see what was going on for quite a distance. But there were also very old, large trees on the sides of the paths. We had the advantage of seeing all movement around us while being screened from the sight of others, especially in the summer. As we left, we did not even whisper but used signs. To say good-bye, for instance, we crossed ourselves—everyone was Catholic, after all. It all looked routine, but each time I left I had the feeling that this was the last time I would see the farm. I would not return to say "Good morning," my happiest expression. I began to lose hope that the war would ever end.

We received information on the war in several ways. From time to time we received the Underground Bulletin. This was a small paper, mimeographed or printed on a hand press. Occasionally someone would bring in a newspaper from Vilnius, in either German or Polish-language Lithuanian. They were well accepted by most, since toilet paper was not available. In conversation with German officers on the farm I congratulated them on their victories on the Eastern front and showed them the articles I had read. They showed little reaction. I also read how many Allied ships and submarines had been sunk by the Germans. It seemed that more of them were torpedoed and sunk than the Allies ever built.

I pretended never to be interested in politics. I talked only of the victories, about which I read in the newspaper. I could not talk about German setbacks because there were none. In time, the officers, especially the first two I met, became friendlier, and we began to develop a rapport. Though I could not show any reaction to any information, they started to unburden themselves. The more they talked about setbacks and the real situation, the less interest I showed. I was almost apathetic. When they started talking about the concentration camps, I told them point blank that I did not believe them. I said that it was just propaganda and that it was impossible for Germans to build murder factories. They tried to explain to me why it was being done, and where. I never opened my mouth on the subject. Later, they told me about Hitler's success in eliminating Jews, Gypsies, and Communists. From then on I began to indicate that I believed what was going on. In Germany, it was a known fact. News from other sources trickled into our area little by little about what was happening in the concentration camps, later known as extermination camps, and in the factories where slave labor was flourishing. (After the war, when the German population swore it did not know anything about these, they were simply lying. If low-ranking officers knew, their families must also have known. They were sent home on furloughs and had the opportunity to tell what they knew.)

They never mentioned what really was happening behind the walls of the Vilnius ghetto. That news was spread by the Lithuanians, who were proud of liquidating the Jews from Vilnius. In the city, the year 1942 had at first seemed less chaotic and more hopeful than had 1941. The Jews, though afraid, were selected according to their professions. The tailors, for example, worked in shops organized by the Germans in which uniforms for the German army were sewn or repaired. They worked under tremendous pressure, twelve to fourteen hours a day, while the shops themselves were open twenty-four hours a day. Under the pretext of having been selected for work in Germany, some men, as well as many women and children, were instead sent to Ponary, to be brutally murdered. Many had even volunteered for this type of labor in the hope of improving their misery. Some escapees from Ponary brought the sad news back to the ghetto.

In 1943, the Vilnius ghetto was destroyed. Work permits and other documents were no longer of any value. The remaining few thousands were shipped to concentration camps in Estonia and Latvia. A few hundred escaped east to the woods where Russian partisan groups were active. Unfortunately for the lucky ones not caught during their journey, they were refused unless they possessed some kind of weapon. Those who did had mostly belonged to the organized groups that had been planning an uprising in the ghetto. Those who were not accepted tried to survive in the woods by themselves without any resources during the harsh winters. I was told that some tried to join the Polish Resistance (the Armia Krajowa), but were rejected for being Jewish. I believe that, based on my own experience with the A.K.

When the Germans learned of the escape route from the ghetto through the sewer pipes, they positioned Ukrainian units near the exit and Jews were shot as they emerged.

Some Jews hid in the ghetto behind false walls and in other disguised spaces. Houses with suspicious or inaccessible areas were demolished by the Germans. Those in hiding perished in the rubble. First, though, the Ukrainians had rampaged through the vacated apartments, collecting all of the loot. Once the Germans realized what the Ukrainians were doing, they took over the destruction of the ghetto, collecting all the valuable possessions themselves. And that was the end of the Vilnius ghetto. Of the seventy thousand Jews living there in 1941, only a few thousand registered as survivors after the war.

The German officers who visited the farm repeatedly invited me to their barracks. They knew that my farm administrator would not let me go to see them empty-handed. Without being noticed or appearing to have any interest in the barracks, I tried to memorize the layout, outside entrances, windows, guards, and other details. On one occasion I asked if I could use the toilet because I desperately needed to. They asked one soldier to show me the way. On my return I "got lost," on purpose of course. I displayed a great deal of concern at how stupid I had been by not knowing my way back and how frightened I had become at finding myself in such strange and unfamiliar surroundings. Another time I fell, ensuring that my hands became very dirty in the process, so I could ask to go somewhere to rinse them. After a while I became more familiar with the place, having learned its layout, customs, and procedures. I was pleased to see that security was very lax for an army establishment.

I noticed some Russian POW's performing dirty work, along with civilians. I never learned who they were. They did not look like the farmer-peasants from the area, but more like slave workers imported from elsewhere. I never heard them talking, so I could not tell what language they spoke.

After a while, some of the soldiers knew that I always brought goodies, but not for them. They knew me as "Josef, the fisherman from the farm." They even approached to see if they could purchase some fresh farm products from me. I always replied that I wished I could have gotten some for myself, but that I was afraid to steal. In turn, I was becoming increasingly envious of many things they possessed. Bartering, however, was too dangerous. It also would have been impossible during my short visits to the

barracks. Nevertheless, I considered the idea, even discussed it a few times during my visits with my contact in
Vilnius.

My contact very much wanted to plan a daring night-
time attack on the barracks, to be carried out by an experienced unit from another area. He would choose the
people; that way, whether successful or not, suspicion
would not be directed at us. I considered this plan unrealistic, but he insisted that a similar action worked very successfully in another location, with only "minor casualties."
To my question, he replied that "minor casualties" meant
a few people slightly injured. He had not said where the
action had taken place, so I did not ask. The implication
was that I should not know, and I knew it was better for
me not to.

I explained that to approach the barracks the unit
would have to travel a long way through very dangerous
terrain occupied by the Lithuanians, not to mention the
Germans. They would have to retrace their route or find
another, with their booty, after everyone had been alerted
by the attack. It would be a long time until they were able
to unload the arms they seized. Some of it would have to
be transported to us later. The only safe routes were
through the woods, but there were many difficulties moving such heavy traffic through them with only a few wagons. I told him bluntly that his plan would lead to disaster.

On the other hand, I did not sincerely believe that my
alternative plan would work either. I had such limited resources. I put all my trust in luck. I finally received permission and orders to act on my own. I had been planning to set up a small-scale action without fanfare. I
wanted to enlarge our "arsenal," which was limited and

mainly for our own use. Summer was closing in on us, so we had to act quickly. Fall's muddy ground would make it impossible.

One cloudy and stormy night a small wagon, well loaded with straw and pulled by the best horse on the farm, was prepared for me. I wore ragged old shoes. They had been lying, dusty, by the rye bin as long as I could remember. If someone had to step into the bin he was supposed to wear them instead of his regular shoes, normally dirty from the barn. However, I never noticed anyone actually using them and decided to appropriate them for my purposes. My own boots had pieces of an old tire nailed to the bottom for indestructible soles. But the tire had a particular tread; and if someone investigated, its impression on the ground could easily be identified and traced. Upon returning from this action, I threw the shoes I had appropriated into the latrine and covered them with a little dirty straw. No one ever noticed their disappearance or asked for them. Two empty milk containers, used for delivering milk to the depot, were also loaded onto the wagon and covered with straw.

I quietly took off through the fields. These were rough rye fields, mowed and used as cattle pastures. Two strong, muscular fellows, who did not live on our farm or even in our area, were waiting for me on the edge of the forest by a side road. Without a word they jumped onto the wagon. They had two rifles which they carried in a sack, like potatoes. If we had to use them, we knew that our escapade would end unsuccessfully. We took them only in case we should encounter a problem on the road, or if we should have to run and cover our retreat.

We headed past the barracks, then made a large circle back to approach it from the far end. We parked the wagon some distance away behind wild bushes. One man stayed with the horse and wagon while two of us went quietly toward the barracks. I headed for the place where a window was always kept open in the summertime. It was ajar. I opened it very slowly, unsure if it would squeak or make some other noise. So far, that was the easy part of the job. My partner made a stirrup of his hands and boosted me up as I held his shoulder. I swung a leg over the window frame, looking for solid footing, then pulled the other foot in. This was much like the exercises I had performed for my training as a fireman.

Inside was easy. I had only to watch not to step on something or make any noise. The room I was in looked like a small barn hall. I thought I was in a storage room. With the dim light of my flashlight I was surprised to see all kinds of cans, some metal and wooden parts, old uniforms, and other junk. There were few weapons, to my disappointment. I grabbed two rifles not knowing whether they were rejects awaiting repair or were in good shape. I handed them to the fellow outside who ran with them to the wagon. When he returned I handed him a few hand grenades that had been lying on a table, as if on display. I returned a second time to pick up the rest of the grenades. When I looked outside he hadn't returned. I was afraid to toss them out the window in case of noise. So I waited. What must have been seconds dragged on like long minutes. I could not understand what had happened. I was about to grab only the two that I could hold in one hand when he arrived. I passed him the load, keeping one in my hand. I could not resist the temptation to grab a blanket that I had noticed at the last moment. Holding the grenade and blanket close to my body with one arm I negotiated the window with my one free hand. I slid down my partner's shoulder to the ground. The moment we reached the wagon the driver slowly started. We hid everything under the straw.

Later, I learned from its label that the blanket had been made in Holland for the Dutch troops that served alongside the German army. I was considering making winter underwear out of it, but I didn't have the heart to cut up such a fine possession. It was light as a feather, soft and fluffy — not like a standard army blanket. I removed the label, to eliminate any traces of its origin. I made spots on it with berries, to make it look old and dirty. Actually, I deceived only myself. I stuffed it into my straw "mattress" to cover the straw and keep it from poking me through the sackcloth. From then on I slept like a king, especially during the winter nights when the cold penetrated from the clay floor. I became so attached to it that I kept it through the war and took it with me when I returned to Poland in 1945.

The two rifles, though without ammunition, were the best ones we had. The risks we took in this escapade had been worthwhile. German hand grenades (the kind with the handles for throwing) were a great treasure for us. They were easy to carry in our boots and easy to grab when necessary. Though they were not very accurate when thrown from a distance and did not do as much damage as we would have liked, they were excellent when used for surprise at the beginning of an attack. We threw them from opposing directions to confuse the enemy. They also served us as land mines, since we did not have actual mines. We would place one in the road and cover it up. We attached a string to the firing pin, which was pulled by someone in hiding. He would then escape to the woods.

After leaving the barracks, we headed home as quickly

as possible. On our way we unloaded one of the men, who quickly took off in another direction to some other village. The two of us continued to the place where the second man kept his "supplies" and unloaded the wagon. His responsibility was to wrap the other gear and to store it in a safe place. I returned to the farm empty-handed, for security. The arrangements we had made this time were that, if I had not returned by late morning, another man from our farm, the one who usually delivered milk, would go to the collection depot. After delivering the milk, he would ask why I had not returned saying that I had been supposed to deliver the milk instead of him that day.

The day passed normally, with no one realizing anything had happened. We did not hear any news from the village, either. The next morning two Germans came to hunt, as they did from time to time. They acted normally, but their moods were not cheerful and happy; instead, they were stiff and serious. As they were leaving without any game, I wished them better luck next time. I suggested that they should not be upset at such a minor thing. At that moment, Tadeusz was passing by on the way to the barn. He greeted them and I explained why they were upset. He invited them inside and asked me to assist them, although I was supposed to finish the work I was doing. (I had been stacking firewood — the only fuel we had — beside the hut for winter. Freshly cut and split wood needed to dry outside.) Tadeusz ordered the maid to prepare some eggs and ham with bread. It made me uncomfortable to watch them devour food that I had been craving and while so many others were dying from hunger. During our conversation I asked them if something bothered them or if they had had some bad news from home. I did not dare to ask them if there was anything wrong on the front. That sort of thing was not supposed to interest me, though they volunteered information themselves once in a while.

This time they took me in their confidence and asked if I could be of any assistance by snooping around. Though I was only a worker, they considered me the only trustworthy friend they had among the population. When I asked about the Lithuanians who worked so closely with the German army, they expressed their disdain with a strong, obscene description. They told me, privately, that during the previous night some thieves had broken into their barracks and committed a burglary. I asked if they had taken a small or a large sum of money. They had not stolen money, I was told. Food from the kitchen? No. Some Communists had stolen guns. "Guns from the soldiers?" I asked. "You must be kidding me. I don't believe it. It is impossible."

The Germans said that it must have been some of the POW's or the workers who knew exactly where and what was being stored in the room on that day. They were certain to find them. From the crumpled weeds they knew that there must have been quite a few of the Bolshevik partisans who had been operating from the woods in the area. Sooner or later they would be destroyed. I asked how it could be possible for someone to steal with so many soldiers always moving around the barracks. They shook their heads. They were sure that the information came from someone who knew the barracks. Also, they were sure that the thieves came through the wild side of the barracks and through the window, because when they had escaped they left the window wide open.

I asked, seeming naive, why they thought I could help? I did not know anyone in that part of the country. Didn't they realize how little the farmers in the area liked the "people on the hill"? The Germans said that they were sure some peasants must have been among the gang because they found their footprints in the sand and only that type of scum wore such ragged shoes. I asked if, by any chance, some Lithuanians couldn't have been included in this gang because some nights we heard shots. People said they came from Lithuanian militiamen on drunken rampages.

I was told to be quiet, not to tell anyone what had happened, and to keep my ears open. If I learned anything or heard anything suspicious, I knew where to find them. Talk only to them and I would be well rewarded. During their later visits the events of that night were never again mentioned. I did express fear and concern that those bandits might someday come to our farm to steal everything. Who knew, I said, they might even hurt us for working for the Germans.

One time I was informed that the priest was to be arrested. I assumed this meant he would be sent somewhere never to return. This took me by surprise, though I kept my poker face as I usually did when I wanted to show my indifference to a message. I did not say anything, though the tall one, who usually did the talking, stopped for a moment as if he wanted me to ask why. At that point I wondered why he was telling me this. Did he know anything about my past that he should not have known? Was he fishing for a reaction? My fears were unnecessary; he said the priest was spreading anti-German propaganda from the pulpit in his sermons.

They knew I attended the church almost every Sunday and listened to the sermons. What was he saying? I strongly disagreed with his accusation, saying that I could tell him exactly what the priest was preaching because I was even helping him, from time to time, with his sermons. He had books of sermons that he repeated word for word. I told him that the priest was such an old man that he was even scared of his own shadow. He would never say a word against the Germans because he always said they had helped him to recover the church and its land after the Communists had nationalized them. It was well known that I had helped him recover it all for the church with the assistance of the German authorities.

That afternoon I sneaked out to the parish. I had a quiet, short talk with him and the curate and told them what had happened. The priest was never arrested or even interrogated by the authorities. What the Germans did not know, however, was that they had the right information — but about the wrong man. It was the curate (*vikary*) who sometimes gave sermons filled with strong political views, telling people how it really was. The Germans must have gotten incorrect information from an informer. After this incident the curate — though young, daring, and forceful — changed his tune.

The visits of the officers continued, though it was customary for them to rotate. Every one of them was afraid to be sent to the Eastern front. This was also the penalty for any misbehavior. I called them "my heroes"; they called me "our friend Josef." In time they became more open and talkative. The most interesting information was about the traffic to and from the Eastern front. They never did tell me the exact purpose of the military barracks, but they knew exactly when to expect convoys and what kind they would be. This type of information was the most valuable, and I could obtain it easily. I passed all of this to my contact. While I am certain that the Germans used many different routes to the front, the one near us was always the same. Knowing exact dates helped our larger, better-organized, and better-equipped units down the road to be more successful.

The time came when the Germans even started using Russian vehicles. These were fueled with gasifiers: kettles filled with wood chips, covered by rattling lids, from whose tops rose chimneys made of pipe. I did not know how to interpret what I saw. Perhaps it was the beginning of the end, or perhaps they were only saving the limited supply of gasoline for use on the front lines. It definitely did not look impressive for the mighty German army to be using old Russian wood-fueled half-tracks.

The Germans had previously issued a decree demanding that by a particular date anyone possessing a fur coat, collar or shawl, anything made of fur, whether for men or women, even a tiny piece, must turn it in at specially designated depots—under penalty of death. This was posted mostly in the cities. People assumed that the furs would be sent to Germany for the civilian population. The farmers didn't even consider turning in their sheepskin coats, made from skins they had tanned themselves.

On our farm we had the big, loose overcoat with an attached hood, made from white sheepskins. It was used only by the privileged when making a trip during harsh winters. It was long and very heavy. Walking in it was very clumsy. Immediately after the confiscation order was issued, Tadeusz, the farm administrator, went to Vilnius and obtained a permit allowing us to keep the coat for the farm's use. The permit was typed, and stamped and signed on a small piece of cloth that had to be sewn to the coat.

Previously, when the German soldiers had plundered Jewish properties, they had shipped all the furs (mainly women's coats and silver fox shawls, which were then in style) to their families. But on one bitter winter day we saw troops riding east in open trucks wrapped in all kinds of women's fur coats and shawls — even fur muffs for their hands! We could not believe our eyes. The mighty army now looked like a group of the condemned, shivering from the cold.

As we realized that the Germans were beginning to lose the war, we started to gain self-confidence. Our egos grew, and we felt enthusiasm about everything we were supposed to do. We increased our subversive activities, still always in a "no-man's land" very far from our village. Unfortunately, the unexpected could still happen. We were trapped one night and had to bury two of our members. Their loss was one of my most upsetting experiences. A few of us were in the woods as backups for those who went into action by the high road. They daringly revealed themselves to the Germans instead of operating from behind cover, as they had been instructed. We heard a large number of salvoes and realized they had not come from our people. Before we could size up the situation, we were happy to hear our people returning — until we noticed that they were dragging two bodies. It was hard to accept, a blow to us all, especially as it was the first time that anything like this had happened. The two who were killed were our most daring. I did not know what to do. There was nothing but to bury our lost comrades quickly. The soil was frozen but sandy enough that we were able to leave them in shallow graves. Their families were informed that the Lithuanian militia had arrested them for an unknown reason and turned them over to the Germans, who then shipped them to Germany for work at a farm, factory, or some other facility. The peasants could believe it because these things had happened before. Only after it was safe (I heard later) were the families told what had really happened and where the graves were so they could rebury their men with a religious ceremony.

During our hurried "funeral" in the woods, my father's parting words flashed into my mind, "Do everything that you are supposed to do, and do it well, but don't try to be a hero." I had understood then from the way he moved his head that he had meant "a dead hero," but he would not or could not say it.

We tried to take anyone injured during an action inconspicuously to our village physician, our only resource. He was on our side and was a tremendous help. He supplied all necessary medications insofar as his limited supply allowed. By helping us, he was endangering his own life and that of his wife, who assisted him when necessary, because he was supposed to report any injury to the authorities. He reported our injuries as farm accidents.

With the coming of spring 1944, we heard rumors that the German army was suffering large losses on the Eastern front, even larger than those of the winter. The melting snow and thawing ground made the soil muddy. Heavy armor and other equipment would get stuck in the mud and be impossible to maneuver. Much the same disaster that had befallen Napoleon's army happened to the Germans.

The visits of German officers to our farm became less and less frequent. Sometimes they would mention that they were regrouping for a final offensive on Moscow. We knew what that meant: each time the army had to withdraw, it was always a "strategic maneuver." Their faces showed worry — never a joke or a smile. They never mentioned or admitted the disaster that was happening on the front. Finally, they stopped coming at all and we no longer had any contact with them. They may have been sent to the front, as was most of the available German manpower.

Suddenly, all the convoys and traffic, which had been moving east, started moving west. The papers said that these were only temporary strategic regroupings amidst great victories; unofficially, I was told that the Germans were losing the war, were retreating and fleeing west.

Soon afterwards, a courier came to me with a code. I had been waiting for years. After I explained the code to Tadeusz, I called upon the forester, with his knowledge and permission. I went under the pretext of obtaining a permit that would allow us to cut a certain number of square meters of timber from the woods and haul it back to the farm. I had to see the forester personally to confirm the validity of the code, as had been previously arranged. The code read: "Come out from underground. Bear arms openly. Wear an identification armband. Engage cautiously. Further orders will follow." He suggested that I not use a horse, but go on foot so as not to arouse suspicion. He also feared that some German soldier might confiscate a horse, no matter what kind of documents I had or to whom the horse might belong. They were already desperate for any kind of transportation. Though it was quite a long trip each way I was so excited that I did not mind walking and marched along quickly. It is hard to describe the excitement when we regrouped as an organized unit. The farmers were astonished to see their own sons in Polish, German, or Russian uniforms, but all wearing identical armbands and carrying arms.

We did not start charging the Germans, as everyone in their excitement wanted to do. There still were more of them, better trained and much, much better armed. There-fore, we kept to the old strategy: hit and run. But now the Germans did not have the time or ambition to pursue us. Their distraction, the element of surprise, and our loca-tions for ambush were the few advantages we had. We now operated in the daytime, usually in hilly areas from behind embankments that concealed us. We did not save ammunition as we had before; we used whatever we had, not worrying about where we would get more. Some of our men obtained automatic weapons, which we had not had previously. I did not want to know exactly how they were obtained, though I knew they had belonged to Ger-man soldiers and were obtained at great risk to their own lives.

German soldiers, as individuals or very small groups, started drifting on foot into the villages. They confiscated food from farmers and requisitioned horses and buggies for transportation. They were easy targets for us. We spread ourselves around our village and the two adjoin-ing ones, awaiting the unwanted guests. We were also provided additional equipment, which was useful. The fearful farmers, most of whom were poor peasants, treated us as royalty and shared with us whatever we needed. I did not eat during the war years as well as I did during that time.

A few days later the forester came charging into the village on a horse looking for me. He was wearing an army uniform, the first time I had seen him in one. He had the rank of major. When I realized that, I saluted him. He returned the salute and, also for the first time, we ex-changed friendly smiles. The major told me that the Rus-sian army was in the area, and that we were all to report the next day before noon to a particular location. It was an open area surrounded by forest. We were to avoid main roads and highways, as the Russians would be using them. Finally, he informed me that he had petitioned for my promotion to captain and that I would formally receive that rank later. His congratulations were the last I heard of it, as shortly afterwards I would lose all contact with the A.K.

We quickly assembled, said good-bye to the villagers, got food for the road, and set out on our way. During the night we became tired and decided to sleep for a few hours. We changed sentries every half-hour. To keep track of the time, at each change of watch the guards handed an actual watch to the next ones. We resumed our march at daybreak.

Suddenly I saw three Russian soldiers approaching on horseback. At first I thought they were partisans from the socialist People's Army (Armia Ludowa), which I, as a member of the National Army, had always tried to avoid. I realized that since there were more of us than them this time, they would not start any trouble. But when I got a closer look, I realized that they were not partisans but regular soldiers in Russian uniforms. As soon as they noticed the armbands on our clothing they knew who we were. We exchanged a few compliments, though I was sure that none of them were sincere. Their leader asked if we had seen any Germans, as some were still in the area. I replied disdainfully that if we had seen any there wouldn't be any now. He then noticed the German revolver in my holster and asked if I wanted to exchange it for his Russian automatic rifle. I had always dreamed of having this kind of small automatic rifle with a round magazine attached like a small drum. I agreed to the exchange. He asked me to show him the revolver. I removed it from the holster, pointing out to him that I wanted to see his weapon. He made no move, saying that he would give it to me after examining my revolver. I put it back into my holster and we both smirked, knowing neither of us trusted the other. With him on horseback and me on foot, I was thinking, what could I do if he grabbed my gun and rode away? Try to chase him on foot? Take a gun from one of my men and start a shoot-out with Russian soldiers? No. We parted as "friends," knowing what each of us had in mind.

Before noon we arrived at our destination. The place was crowded, bustling with a few hundred men dressed in all kinds of uniforms and carrying a motley assortment of weapons. We reported to one of the officers in charge of the entire group. Everyone was still identified by his code surname and not by his real name or rank. Most of us did not wear any rank insignia. A young sergeant who looked like a bull approached me and said there would be a parade and review of all the units. Each unit was to be prepared to march in proper army style. The whole company would be reorganized to fight alongside the Russian army, but under our own command. At noon a mass was going to be conducted and per the commander's orders, our unit had been chosen to build and prepare an altar. Surprised, I opened my eyes and asked, "With what?" He snapped back, "Are you a Jew and don't know how to organize an altar?" I froze for a moment, but knew I had to react and said angrily, "For such language I should knock your teeth out, but I can't because I respect your uniform." He gave me a dirty look and walked away without saying a word. I was satisfied with my own conduct in the situation; I had acted as a paper tiger.

Immediately I directed two of my men to head in opposite directions and find some farm hut. I was sure that they would find a crucifix because almost every farmer had one hanging on a wall. They were to borrow it and bring it back as quickly as possible. In the meantime, others gathered tree limbs. They constructed a table, lashing the limbs with soft twigs. We covered it with a blanket. In the same way, we made two large crosses and stuck them in the ground on either side of the table. The men cut some grass and spread it on the tables. They also found wildflowers to decorate the rough blankets covering them. One man returned, running, with a crucifix, which we attached to some wood to keep it standing. (The other man found a large one, but not until the short mass was over.)

I then took my men aside and showed them how to march in formation, without martial music. They were to use a half-goose step, not like the Germans. They had to lift their legs only forty-five degrees and keep their hands at the side of their pants, not swinging. When I gave them the order "look right" they were to turn their heads in unison and keep them turned until we passed the "reviewing stand." I told them to keep their rifles, whatever kind they were, hanging from their shoulders to keep their hands free. We practiced this for a few minutes, and I hoped for the best.

The parade went better than I had expected. Someone beat a marching cadence on an old, small drum. I do not know where he had found it, but it did the trick. The drummer stood to the left of the makeshift reviewing stand, so as we approached we could hear him well. I marched to the right of our first column. When I approached the "dignitaries" I barked out the order and saluted as I faced them. The men moved smartly and I was complimented later. The men were pleased and proud of themselves, too, as this was the first time they had ever marched in formation.

After the parade, we were all happy and full of hope but didn't know what to do with ourselves. Many napped in the shadow of the woods, as it was already hot for the middle of June. Some sat around in small groups and chewed the fat. We waited, not knowing what we were waiting for. Finally, later in the afternoon, came the signal for all to assemble.

One of the senior officers said a few words praising our achievements, but then warned us that he had unpleasant news. Our top brass had not come to an agreement with the Russian generals. The Russians would accept us only under the condition that we integrate into the People's Army and serve under Russian command. The officer strongly suggested (it sounded like an order, but it did not have to be obeyed) that we spread out and head west, towards Warsaw, to help our army liberate that city from the Germans. Anyone who would not do this should go home, hide his weapons, and await further orders.

Disappointment was clear on every face. I took my group to the side and explained that, as individuals, we had no chance to reach Warsaw. It was a long distance on foot, and the Russians were said to be everywhere. We might even come across some Germans. I suggested that they make their way home at night, hide their weapons, and pretend nothing had happened, living their lives as normally as possible. I would contact them when things changed. I could not return to the village, because the Russians would find me.

Some soldiers started to drift away, either home or to the west. Not long afterwards there was a rush and commotion. Before I could size up the situation, we were surrounded by a swarm of Russian soldiers. Some had short automatic rifles, and some had their rifles with bayonets affixed aimed at us. I could not understand what was happening or why we had not been warned by our sentries. I could hear our officers shouting orders not to shoot. I felt like a chicken in a cage—I am sure that others did also. I assumed that this was some mistake or misunderstanding.

Our officers exchanged heated words with the Russians, then told us to form a single line and turn in all our weapons. They repeated it: put all weapons and ammunition onto the three small Russian army trucks that had driven in. Slowly, we did as we had been told. This looked like an unconditional surrender to our "allies," the greatest humiliation we could imagine. All of us, including the officers, were then ordered to march, under guard to an unknown destination. It was late in the evening when we came to an open area, surrounded by an old chicken-wire fence that was partially supported by high wooden boards. It looked as if it might have been previously used by the Germans as some sort of storage depot. We unpacked our blankets and other belongings. Some Russian soldiers were digging a deep pit that, I later learned, was to serve as our latrine. Later that evening we each received a thick slice of dark bread. The Russians unloaded a few barrels of water as well.

I was tired and tried to sleep under the night sky, but to no avail. It was noisy, and I kept thinking about what would come next. Perhaps the Russians would deport us to Siberia, as they had done with so many thousands of "undesirables." I fell asleep repeatedly, but always awoke to a clear sky with bright stars shining.

Good Morning

Finally, in the morning, they had us assemble and, in Russian, explained: the Russians were our friends; they had liberated us, sustaining much damage and many casualties. Much Russian blood had been shed in the fields. They equipped and trained the People's Army which fought alongside them and were, even now, liberating Poland on their way to take Warsaw from Nazi hands. We were welcome to join them in this task — or we could be shipped to labor camps in Siberia. We would be given time to make up our minds. The army did not feed parasites: to join the People's Army was our only choice.

A great commotion ensued. We were shocked, confused, and surprised. It appeared that no one would join the Communist army. Later in the afternoon, bread and soup was brought in army kettles. Everyone rushed to the area where food was distributed. The Russians had a hard time keeping order, even though the rush was to help those who were distributing the food.

Just then, I had an idea how we might escape. After struggling to get my rations, I moved to the corner opposite the food with my two men, Janek and Tolek Jankowski. We laid our blankets in the corner next to the fence and I explained my plan. It was risky, but could work and was the best I could figure out. That night we would dig a hole under the fence, big enough for us to crawl through. We would escape when everyone was occupied with the food distribution.

Of course, everything was harder and more complicated than I had imagined. We had no tools with which to dig. The best implements we could find were pieces of wood and a stone. Our hands were hard from farm work, but not hard enough. We took turns under a blanket digging mostly with sticks through the black soil. The blanket hid the loose dirt.

Finally the hole was large enough for us to crawl under the fence. We left a thin layer of grass on the other side to be removed at the last minute, so that our hole would not be seen from the other side. I planned to break through the next day during the turmoil of food distribution, then crawl and run toward a barn we could see in the distance. The pack with the rolled-up blanket would be tied to my foot so I could pull it after me. If I did not get caught and saw that the way was clear, I would signal Janek, the older brother, to follow. Tolek would help Janek crawl through, pushing if necessary, as he was a little on the heavy side.

At the planned time, I went, giving the hand signal to follow when I had gone about twenty yards. I ran as fast as I could, stooped, with the bundle pressed to my stomach. I looked back and saw Janek partially through the hole, which reassured me. I did not look to see if I had been spotted. When I reached the barn I opened its big gate slightly but could not see my companions right away. A short time later I spotted both of them running toward me. Once in the barn, our first thought was to hide behind the piles of hay and straw; but we spotted a hole in the ground at the far end, an opening to the cellar. It was only a tunnel at whose end farmers stored potatoes for the winter to keep them from freezing. At this time of the year it was usually partially or completely empty. I signaled the two brothers and crawled down as far as I could. Sandy soil rained down on me whenever I brushed against it. I could feel it on my hands, face, and neck. It worked its way past my collar and down my shirt. Janek and Tolek followed, without a word. Inside was pitch black. The air was heavy and smelled of mildew. We sat down and whispered to each other. Then we crawled out, swapped places so I could take the outermost position, and crawled back waiting for nightfall.

Not long afterwards we heard the opening of the barn gate and the steps of a few people on the clay barn floor running around, searching. Someone must have seen us running toward the barn and reported it. The soldiers must not have seen anything suspicious because one of them shouted in Russian, "We know that you are here. If you do not get out, we will pierce you with our bayonets."

They must have been convinced that we were hiding in the piles of hay and straw. When we did not appear we could hear them talking loudly — on purpose, so that we could hear, "Let's poke the piles with the bayonets. So we will get them dead or alive."

I don't know how many of them there were, but we could hear the activity up in the barn. Quite a while later one of them shouted, "Give me a match and I will set the crop on fire. We will smell them roasting alive."

I relaxed then, because I knew that they would not set the barn on fire. Not only was there danger that fire would spread to some nearby huts with thatched roofs, but also they would not want to harm the peasant who owned the barn, for propaganda reasons. A fire might even set the dry pine woods on fire. I heard, "We can go now; they are not here. If they are, they will roast."

We stayed put in our crowded space. Perhaps twenty or thirty minutes passed when we heard both gates being opened simultaneously and some soldiers charging in, expecting to catch us by surprise. They must have been convinced that we were still hiding in the barn. This time it sounded as if there were many of them. They shouted for us to come out of hiding or be killed. They searched even

more thoroughly, probing piles of hay and straw and anywhere they could find a space. They climbed the wooden
ladder and checked the loft. Suddenly, one of them had
the idea that we might be hiding in the hole, "We know
you are there. Come out with your hands up and nothing
will happen to you."

That was silly. Our weapons had been confiscated. We
could not even straighten our bodies, let alone put our
hands up. Janek was next to me. I felt for his face and put
my hand over his mouth. He understood what I meant. I
was afraid even to breathe, that I might be heard. The
soldiers did not have a light to shine down the hole, and
none of them dared to jump inside. When still nothing
happened, one shouted, "We will shoot you down like
dogs, and this will be your grave!"

Due to the angle of the tunnel, I knew that bullets fired
from the top could not hit us. What I did fear was that
one small man might crawl inside with a light—and that
would be the end of our freedom. As they were leaving,
someone threatened to throw a grenade down the hole.
That did not bother me, either. Nobody in his right mind
would throw a live grenade such a short distance and at
such an angle. He would kill himself and might destroy
the barn. When, finally, all of them left, I assumed that
they had left some sentry at the gates, and that they would
return.

We waited until dusk. I heard the back gates opening.
Someone wheeled in a hand wagon. Slowly, I crawled
out and put my head up to see what was happening. It
was already dim in the barn, so I continued the rest of the
way out of the hole and crept up behind a man facing
away from me. I recognized him as a farmer who was
collecting feed for his animals for the night, part of the

normal routine. When I was close enough I jumped up and put my hand over his mouth. To calm him, I whispered that we were not Germans, nor Russians, nor Lithuanians, but friends who would not harm him as long as he did what I asked.

I asked if there were still Russians around the barn. He seemed surprised at the question. I told him I needed three pairs of pants, the worst he had and the more ragged the better, and two old sacks. He claimed not to have three pairs. I replied that he had the one he was wearing, the one he wore for church on Sunday, and some other, patched, pair. Again, I assured him that the more patches and tears, the better. I promised him in exchange three good pairs of pants, some uniform clothes, and two good blankets, The blankets were a treasure for the farmers, who used them to make all kinds of clothing.

I instructed him to take his wagon to the cattle barn, unload it, and feed his animals as usual, without indicating that anything had happened. Later, he should bring the clothes in an old sack. No one at all should learn of my presence, not even his wife. If he did not do as I said, I would set the barn on fire, pointing to the matches in my pocket (I had none). He became even more fearful and started saying that he did not have any spare clothing for me. I told him to be quiet and that I did not care where he got the pants. If he did not do as I said or told anyone of my presence, I would . . . and pointed at my pocket. He was terrified. All his crops, the fruits of a year's hard labor, were stored there. They were his only possessions, the only way he could feed himself, his family, and his livestock. I rushed him out and repeated: only rags, the worse the better.

I immediately jumped back into the cellar, where we

waited. The minutes dragged as we wondered what would happen. Finally, we heard noises. I peered out of the hole to see the farmer looking for me where the hay was stored. He was carrying a sack over his shoulder. I jumped out and went around the hay so he would not see where I had been hiding. It was already late in the day and dark enough in the barn that you could only make out silhouettes.

The farmer had brought what I wanted, even better than I had expected. There were pieces of clothing you could hardly call trousers — they were assorted patches in the form of pants. One of them was made out of sack-cloth; the others had brown patches made from old socks. I grabbed a pair and told him that the other men would pick theirs up, leaving the good stuff under the hay by the gate. I warned him, again, that if he ever mentioned anything, even later, it would be the end of his farm. We had our people in the area who would get even with him. The Russians might even finish him for helping us. He assured us of his cooperation by crossing his heart.

After he left we quickly changed our clothing. It was already too dark to see how we looked, but we found that all of the clothes were too big and too long. We had to use our belts to keep them from falling down and had to roll the trouser legs up. I tore mine shorter. We bundled up our own clothes and hid them as I had promised. (We only left one blanket, though. I could not part with the other. It was too good and the only booty I had left. It had served me well before and did again later.) Then we jumped back into the hole and waited until it was completely dark.

One by one we sneaked out of the barn. We could see each other by the light of the bright moon in a clear sky.

Good Morning

We looked like dirty clowns or the lowest beggars. I carried an old potato sack on my shoulder in which I kept my blanket. We knew which direction our destination, Vilnius, was in. We could hear some traffic in the distance and assumed it was from the highway. We decided to head toward it. As we approached, we saw a procession of all kinds of Russian army vehicles headed in one direction: toward Vilnius. We lay down in the adjoining field and waited for daybreak.

The next morning we approached the highway, looking like bent, dirty, tired, slave laborers, just as we wanted. We tried to stop some vehicles, but had no success. We started to walk, very slowly, at the extreme edge of the road, trying to avoid either sliding into the ditch or getting run over. We walked with the traffic, occasionally signaling that we wanted a ride. Finally, a lone half-track stopped. A man sitting next to the driver asked what we wanted. Tolek, who spoke the best Russian, said in a tired voice, "We have been slaves on a farm. The Germans beat us and forced us to work day and night. Now you have liberated us from slavery and we would like to go home to our families. We are very hungry, very tired, and we can't walk any more. Please take us with you to Vilnius."

The man whispered to the driver then motioned us to hop in the back. He told us that they were not allowed to give rides to civilians. He would have to drop us off before we reached the city because there were sentries at the tollgate in front of it. We thanked him and tried to climb up into the back. Two soldiers, who had heard our plea, were there sitting on some sacks. In keeping with our "exhaustion," we asked the soldiers to help us up. They reached out and pulled us to the floor of the truck. Tolek gave them a good story, saying we were on the verge of collapse and asking if they had a sip of water for us. One of the soldiers gave us some lukewarm water in a tin cup, which he got from the front passenger. We shared it; it tasted very good. Under the circumstances, anything would have.

The two soldiers listened to our story. After some conversation, one reached into a sack on which they had been sitting. He pulled out a loaf of bread and gave it to us. We tore into it like wolves, only then realizing how hungry we actually were. In no time nothing was left, although it tasted like clay. We felt happy and so did the soldiers, seeing how we had gobbled down the food. They told us to lie down so we would not be seen by any passing vehicles. The floor was hard, so we felt every bump and shake. I realized how little padding I had between my skin and bones. The sack with my blanket was of no help. But all this was still better than walking.

The truck stopped long before we reached the city and we had to get out. After it had disappeared from sight we started to walk normally, no longer having to pretend that we were dead tired. We marched happily, knowing we would shortly reach Janek and Tolek's home in Vilnius. For me, it was just another temporary stop.

When we had openly left the farm, as soldiers, their mother came to me and made me responsible for their welfare. She said, "They are the only things I have left in my life." When we reached their home and Janek knocked on the door, their mother opened it silently and cautiously — then slammed it when she saw us. Janek told her who we were, though, and there was a scene of much joy. Their mother had been sure they had been sent to Siberia for hard labor. These were the rumors when she had escaped herself when the Communists arrived at the farm. She sincerely thanked me for delivering her sons.

Good Morning

We took off our filthy clothing. Janek and Tolek's mother warmed water for us and took the rags outside to burn. We washed in a tub and rinsed from a bucket. It felt good to be clean again. I got a set of clean underwear and one of their father's outfits. He had been executed by the Bolsheviks at Katyń. His clothes fit me pretty well.

We spent the rest of the day in pleasant surroundings catching up. They would not let me leave that day, but after a good night's sleep and breakfast, I said good-bye. They assured me that I could return any time and that their house would always be open to me. That meant a lot, given the times and my situation. But it was the last time I ever saw Janek and Tolek.

CHAPTER SIX
❧❧

I went looking for my friends, the Rzadkowski family who lived on Mickiewicza Street. When I found them, I received another warm welcome and was given a room which I shared with their son, Wladziu. (He later died of tuberculosis, despite the medicine I was sending him from the United States.) The father was not there. He had gone out of the city to get food from a farmer whom he knew. His background also made it unsafe for him to be in town. He had been a professional accountant in the army before 1939.

I wanted to go home to my family, hoping for the miracle that I might be reunited with them, but the trip was impossible. The war was still going on, and the front lines were slowly moving west. My home town was still in German hands; to reach it, I would have to go through the Russian and German lines plus the war zone between.

Food and everything else in the city was in very short supply. The little that was available was rationed, with coupons given only to those who worked. The old Russian saying, "*Nie robotash, nie kushash*" (If you don't work, you don't eat) remained the Communist slogan. Even with ration coupons one had to wait in long lines for hours when some produce became available. Usually, however, unless one started near the front of the line, the merchandise would be sold out by the time one's turn came.

Communist party members had their own stores, supposedly stocked with all kinds of goods that they could obtain without limitation. This was also the reason that those same goods were available on the black market, but who could afford them? Definitely not me.

I was sharing whatever food the Rzadkowski family could scrounge. The only solution was for me to go to work and become an official city resident until I could travel west. I learned that in Vilnius the only active graphics firm was Spindulys. They printed newspapers, magazines, as well as other literature and forms for the Russian Army. The company was managed and owned by the Lithuanian Propaganda and Information Ministry. I went there looking for a job in the zincography department, because that was what I knew best. I was disappointed to hear that there were not any openings and kept asking about other departments, but the answer was the same. Finally I asked if they had any positions at all. The only job they had was that of a cutter in the finishing department. I said that I would take it, promoting my skills by telling them that I had been a bookbinder all my adult life. They gave me a piece of paper, written in confusing Lithuanian that I could not decipher, and told me to take it to the director. I later learned that he was a Communist party member, without any knowledge of the profession or the graphics industry.

The director asked me where I had worked before. I already knew from my previous experiences how to deal with a Communist. I told part of the truth: that I had worked in a printing plant, that our family was very poor, and that, as a result, I had performed all kinds of jobs in the plant to make a living. I was a very good student and a very good worker, so I was chosen by a charitable organization to receive a full scholarship to the Graphic Institute in Vienna. I was hungry there, but I had a good opportunity to learn a profession. Before the Germans came to Austria in 1938 I had to flee home. I was afraid of the Nazis because everyone at the Institute knew of my leftist convictions. The director listened attentively, without interrupting, because he had not heard of the Institute in Vienna and because my story seemed to interest him. He asked me what my father was doing (a typical question from a Communist, to learn if one was a bourgeois). I answered that all his adult life he had worked very hard as a printer to provide bread for the family. (Of course, I never mentioned that this was his own plant of forty people. That would have made him a capitalist and, therefore, a foe of the Communists.) I also said that when the Germans attacked my hometown they arrested him, and, since then, I had lost contact with him, while I had had to escape from the Nazis, which was how I came to Vilnius (I said Vilnius rather than Wilno because Lithuanians hated anyone using the Polish name for the city. They did not acknowledge that Vilnius was ever anything but Lithuanian.)

I continued, saying that when the Russian army was in Vilnius in 1940 I was working on a construction site for a printing plant for the Propaganda Ministry. It was never finished due to the war. I showed him some documents from that time which supported my claim. He seemed to know something about the building but did not say anything. I concluded, telling him that when the Germans occupied the city they grabbed me and sent me to the farm in Rukojnie where I had been a slave laborer for three years, and showed him my palms. My story must have convinced him because, without further questions, he sent me upstairs to the foreman on the top floor.

I reported to the foreman, handing him a scrap of paper on which a few words of Lithuanian were scribbled (the other side was an old German form). He read it and looked at me suspiciously, probably thinking that I was a Communist because I had been sent straight from the director's office. On the other hand, I suspected him of being a Communist because of his position.

He took me to my station and explained that every minute of my work had to be recorded on my time sheet, indicating the job number and the corresponding procedure. I looked around, seeing eight paper guillotines standing in a row. Mine was number eight. The foreman told me what to do, and I energetically started working. At first, I was very careful because any spoilage was considered by the Communists to be sabotage, a charge with grave consequences. I went home happy that afternoon, at the end of my shift, looking forward to payday and, even more, to the food coupons.

On the second day of my job we were cutting stacks of printed sheets into individual ration coupons. Some Russians in army uniforms were present, watching to see that no one tried to steal any. When I got into a discussion with one of the inspectors, an unusually tall man for the Russians, I told him that he did not have to watch me. I was an honest worker and, moreover, if I wanted to steal I could do so without him realizing it, even with him watching me. He became very stern and said that this was not possible. I told him to watch me carefully for five minutes, but he had to agree that if he caught me it would only be between us. He did not answer but smiled at the thought that anyone could challenge him. I continued to work, but more quickly, just for effect, with him watch-

ing every move I made. After a few minutes I loaded another pile of fresh sheets and started cutting. But before I
started, I wiped my nose with my hand (handkerchiefs
were a bourgeois custom). At the same time, I unobtrusively wet my palm with saliva and took the bar of soap
that was rubbed over the dull cutting blade for smoother
operation. As I moved it across the blade I wiped the pressing bar behind the blade with the saliva. I immediately
started cutting. After the first trim I stopped. I looked into
the inspector's eyes and told him that I already had some
coupons. He looked me over from top to bottom and
asked, "Where?"

I reached under the pressing bar and pulled off a full
strip of coupons, still damp from the saliva. His expression might have made the roof fall. I had to explain how I
had done it. After the coupons were all trimmed and removed, the Russian inspector talked to his companions.
From his gestures I imagined that he was explaining to
them how coupons could be stolen. When the next load
came from the printing department and after each pile
was removed from the guillotine, they all bent over, looking at the bottom of the pressing bar. It looked so funny
that the foreman came to me and asked what they were
looking for.

But on my third day at the plant, an incident occurred
that made me fear for my job—and my freedom. I had
learned that the foreman was not a Communist but a
Lithuanian nationalist. He hated Communists and Poles.
So I let him know that I did not like Communists very
much either. He told me not to work so fast, that I was
breaking the norms, and the same level of work would be
demanded from the others. My efforts to work efficiently
were bringing me animosity instead of praise. But this was

not my only surprise that day.

At mid-morning someone came from the office and started a friendly conversation with me, raising my suspicion and worry. I was even more concerned when the conversation turned to the subject of my past. During the period of rule by the Communists nobody could be trusted. Even family members could not always trust each other.

I pretended I was very busy doing my work and did not want to interrupt it for idle chat, so my answers were very brief. He noticed my attitude and started telling me things about himself. This did not ease my suspicions about him, a person from the office whom I did not know and who came upstairs to talk only with me. Many different thoughts came to my mind, all negative. Why the conversation?

But when he asked if I had been a bookbinder before, I brushed him off firmly and said, "Don't I perform my job well? Besides, the director knows all about me." I suggested that he learn any further details he wanted from the director himself, implying that I had been politically cleared and that he would learn no more from me. The man appeared to understand my concern and tried to explain, in a cordial manner, the purpose of his visit. As an office clerk, he was the one who received all the daily workers' reports. He entered them into the job cost sheets and the payroll sheet. My reports stood out from the others. They were not scribbled; they looked as if they had been printed. Every minute was accounted for. From the beginning there were no mistakes, and everything looked clearer to him than he would have expected from a novice worker. When he started receiving them he wanted to know who I was.

I repeated to him the same things about my education

that I had told the director. He asked me whether I knew job estimating. I replied that I had learned how to do it but had never actually practiced it; I was always a worker. (That was always the safest answer.) The clerk explained that, since the plant started operating again after the Communists took over, no jobs were ever billed correctly because they did not have an estimator. They simply charged an approximate price. If I could estimate properly he would request my transfer to the office. The pay would be better and the job easier. I told him that I would try because I had learned the theory. He smiled and left.

Later that afternoon the clerk returned, spoke for some time with the foreman, then told me to gather all my belongings (of which I had none) and come downstairs with him to start my new position. He showed me my desk, actually an old table, which was covered with job envelopes. It faced another desk that was piled with all kinds of papers in disarray and that belonged to the plant technical manager. When I was introduced to him, he explained what I was supposed to do. When I asked for the cost tables for the individual procedures, he laughed. If they had had such a thing, they would not have needed me.

After I got settled (which meant I was given a pencil and the wage scale), I went upstairs to the finishing department for some scrap paper. I then asked the technical manager for information, like cost of materials, equipment amortization schedules, and so on. He brushed me off, saying that I would have to figure it out all by myself, but approximate figures would be good enough. The Communists would never know the difference.

Sitting close to him, I learned that he was a Lithuanian nationalist who hated Communists and who did not hide his views. In his desk was a flask that he used quite often—as a pick-me-up, he said. Most orders for the plant came from the military. If they needed an order to be finished quickly, without having to pay for it, they supplied him with refills for the flask.

The supply of electricity from the town was erratic. Even when the plant had power, it was not enough to run the Linotypes (hot-metal typesetting machines) along with the other equipment. They needed a lot of energy to keep the lead molten. When the Linotypes were needed, the big newspaper press was shut down, and vice versa. Therefore, in back of the plant, they installed a stationary steam engine, fueled with coal that heated its huge boiler. You could hear the chug-chug noise of it working, like an old railroad locomotive. The lights pulsed to the same tempo.

Getting coal was always a problem. The director constantly had to call someone at central Party headquarters to get it delivered in army vehicles. He had contacts because the plant was under the authority of the Political Education and Propaganda Ministry. Production of the daily newspaper required that the plant be operating twenty-four hours a day.

One morning the zincographer did not show up for work. I saw the director come to the technical manager's desk to inform him that the zincographer had been arrested for previously collaborating with the Germans. The director pointed to me and left. The manager did not smile—he always looked angry—but he approached me and said that the director had ordered me to go to the zincographic department in the basement and familiarize myself with it.

Whenever a photograph needed to be printed in the

newspaper or magazine, it would be my responsibility to prepare the printing block. There was an apprentice, but I learned that he was of no help. He had started working a short time earlier as a protégé of the director. I now had two jobs, estimating being the less important of the two. This went on for months, with the director repeatedly assuring me that an experienced zincographer would be brought in from Kaunas, the previous capital of Lithuania.

One incident especially struck me. Two Russian air force officers came to the technical manager with some forms to be printed. It was his job to accept and schedule any printing orders. The forms were reports on aircraft performance and fuel consumption. They were supposed to be confidential, as were any forms printed for the Russian military. Since they had run out, the job had to be printed immediately while they waited. After considerable haggling with the manager, who claimed that it was impossible to accommodate them, they took two cans from their pouch and handed them to him. This immediately changed his attitude. He told me to figure the cost for the job, at which the officers said that price did not matter. They needed it immediately and had plenty of rubles with which to pay. They then proved it by showing us a bag filled with paper rubles.

Pretending that I was estimating, I scribbled some figures and added them on an abacus, which served as a computer in those times. I wrote down a figure I had picked in my head and handed it to the manager. Curious, I read the Russian print on the yellow metal can before the manager put it into his desk drawer. I commended the Russian officers on the detailed printed instructions, also featuring diagrams showing how to open the can, warm up the hot dogs inside, and consume the contents.

But why, I asked, were the same instructions in English (which I had not yet learned) on the bottom half of the can? One answered, "When the Americans were short of food, Russia supplied some of it for the American army. The surplus was left in Russia." When I got to the bottom line, however, which I did understand, no other explanations were needed. It said "Product of U.S.A."

A morning came when the technical manager himself did not show up for work. The director announced to everyone that he had been arrested for his earlier collaboration with the Germans. With the director came a young man, a Communist party member, who was introduced as the new technical manager. He knew nothing about printing; I was supposed to help him and train him. This scared me, because I knew that I would be blamed for anything that went wrong. And many things were wrong, but the previous manager had known how to conceal them.

Everyone in the plant was working under pressure and could not wait until his shift was over (I do not recall any women working anywhere in the plant or in the office). The tension could be felt. No one trusted anyone else. Things stayed much the same until the spring of 1945. The front line had moved west until it was nearly to the German border. I felt that the long-awaited time had come for me to return home and reunite with my family. I went to the director and told him that since the Nazis were finally defeated I planned to leave the plant and go home to my family. With a wild look on his face he said that not only was the war still going on, but under the Communist regime, leaving or changing jobs without his permission was unthinkable. It was severely punishable because it was considered sabotage. If I was caught even planning to do so, I might be punished.

I pleaded with him to consider what he would do in my place, but he told me to study communism and the history of the revolution. Nevertheless, he promised that he would locate a replacement for me. I had heard this promise already, a long time before.

I devoted much time to teaching the apprentice in the zincographic department. I did not achieve any success; I would have done better with an untrained farmer. I knew that I would have to leave Vilnius, whatever the consequences.

The family Rzadkowski, with whom I lived, had already made plans to move to Radom, where their relatives lived. They got permits to travel as "repatriates." Civilian travel was restricted to those traveling west with permits. It was easy to obtain one because the Lithuanians wanted to get rid of all the Poles, thereby proving that this was entirely Lithuanian territory. But all the new I.D.s I possessed were issued by the Communist Lithuanian authorities and stated where I worked. Without a job release, it was impossible to get a permit to travel.

A friend of the Rzadkowski family obtained new documents for me, including a repatriation permit, allowing me to travel as far as Radom. The friend himself was supposed to leave Vilnius for the same destination, as soon as he wound up his "business activities." I never learned just what they were. One thing I did know was that he had a great deal of wealth and wanted to take it with him. If the Communists had learned of it, he, his family, and all his acquaintances could have ended up in Siberian labor camps. He sought help from me to smuggle out some gold coins — a great risk.

I discussed it with the senior Rzadkowski, and together

we arrived at a solution. We had a tiny iron stove for cooking that was to be used on the repatriate train. We had heard that the trip might take two to four weeks in a freight train. Everyone was making preparations for the arduous journey. We got some clay and lined the inside of the stove with it. I pressed twenty gold coins into the clay, then covered them with more clay, hoping the heat would not melt the gold. This had to have been the most expensive stove on the train. My travel permit was my reward for the smuggling operation; the owner of the coins was pleased with the idea. (Some time later, Mr. Rzadkowski wrote to me saying how happy the owner of the gold was. He had received all his coins in perfect condition.)

A few days before our departure I moved to a friend's apartment. That was easy, because all my possessions comprised a bundle with some underwear, shirts, and the blanket I still had from the army. I learned from the Rzadkowskis that the day I did not show up for work two militiamen came looking for me. They were told that I had moved out a month ago, supposedly to go home. The militiamen went through the apartment, asking in which room I had lived. They searched it, though they found nothing.

The following day the newspaper came out without any new pictures. There were only three reprinted ones. Shortly afterwards, another man, this one in civilian clothing, came to check if I really had moved out a month ago, asking if they knew where I might be found.

We met at the train station. I was bundled up with my cap pulled low over my face. Carrying my sack, bent over like a cripple, and leaning heavily on a stick that served as a cane, I would not have recognized myself.

The trip from Vilnius to Radom took over three weeks

in a crowded, squalid freight car. From Radom to Kalisz took only two days. All the trains were free, on essentially no schedule, and were crowded with people traveling in all directions. When I arrived in Kalisz, I anxiously went to our apartment in our building, number 6 on the main street, which had been Piłsudski, but which had been changed to Stalin. I rang the bell. As a half-drunk man opened the door, I introduced myself, asking if he knew of any of my family who had lived there. Without a word he slammed the door in my face. I can still hear the loud boom it made. I stood there, astonished, until a woman opened it again. She knew what had happened and said that her father was a crazy drunkard who did not know what he was saying. She explained that she had moved into the apartment with her father after the Germans had vacated it. I asked if I could rent one room from her, but she said that her father would not like it. I replied that it was a big apartment for two people—something I knew, because I had lived there with my family from the time my father had built the building until the war. She let me in and allowed me to go through the apartment with her, except for the room her father was in. I recognized only the furniture in the hallway and the couch in what had been my room. The woman said that the Germans who had lived there during the war took all the furniture and other belongings back with them when they escaped to Germany. She would not rent a room to me but offered to let me sleep on my couch a night or two until I could find some other living space.

I went down to the street to look around. The warehouse that my father had built near the adjoining building was gone. It had been converted into an apartment building. I wanted to run to see uncles, aunts, and cousins from my mother's side of the family (My father's family had lived in Łódź, an industrial city that was the second largest in Poland). But first I went to see the family printing plant, which occupied the entire first floor of our building. None of the faces there were familiar. I introduced myself to the manager. His face turned white. Stuttering, he said, "Your entire family is supposed to be gone. Where did you come from?"

Anxiously, I asked where he had learned that. He started answering me in half words, finally saying that it was something he assumed. He also said that there was a Jewish office in town where I could learn everything, and told me where it was. I immediately ran there.

The office was in a large house in the center of town. Before the war it had belonged to a Jewish family named Apt, but had been taken over by the Germans. When they escaped near the end of the war they took everything from it. The house was later furnished by the American Joint Distribution Committee to accommodate the few survivors, Jews whose houses and apartments had been eagerly occupied by Poles.

The house included a dining area where food was provided for about fifty people. I knew only two of the people there, but most of them knew my family or knew who they were. Unfortunately, they believed that my family had been sent to the Warsaw Ghetto and from there to Auschwitz (Oświęcim). If they had survived they should already have returned to Kalisz.

I was served a meal and was told that, for my own safety, I should move into the house. I went back for my bundle but first stopped at the printing plant again. Somehow, the face of the plant manager looked familiar to me. It bothered me that I could not remember where I had met him before. When I asked him if I might visit the plant, he took me around himself, introducing me to the workers. Some were friendly and pleasant, whether or not sincerely I could not tell. They asked how I had survived. My answers were simple and cautious, playing it safe out of concern for my own security. I said that I had been kept in hiding by a good farmer somewhere in the east. Other faces seemed annoyed that I had returned alive.

The plant was in almost the same condition as when I had left it. It was operating at full capacity. I learned that when the Germans occupied it, they had turned it over to the Wehrmacht for its own use. Then, when the Russians took it over, it was handed to the Communist Polish Ministry of Education and Propaganda. Under the Communists, a printing plant could not operate as a private concern; it was considered a tool of the party.

As he was leading me around, I noticed that the manager was limping, dragging one foot. At once it came to me who he was. His name was Karczmarek. He had owned a one-man printing shop and was one of the hoodlums belonging to the Endek group in Kalisz.

The Endek was a nationalist, racist organization of far-right extremists who hated everyone who was not Roman Catholic, especially Jews. They interfered in private lives and businesses. They infiltrated the army, government, and other organizations and were very active in the universities, especially the one in Poznań. They claimed to be a patriotic organization; nonetheless, many of their members collaborated with the Nazis. They especially endorsed the Germans' actions against Jews.

When we returned to the office, I asked the manager, point blank, for a job in the plant. I could work in any position; I would even work as a maintenance man. I told him what I had done in my last job in Vilnius. Apologetically, he said that as a son of the previous owner, a bourgeois, the Communist party would not allow me to work there, as I might sabotage the plant. I looked him straight in the eye and asked him what had happened to his previous Endek convictions, along with his own small shop.

He realized, then, that I knew about him and his past. He remarked, "Oh, the Germans confiscated it." But he continued, in a whisper, that he would put me on the payroll without my having to work there. It would be safe because his wife and daughter were the only office employees. He opened a drawer and took out a large wheel of yellow cheese. He had gotten it that day for a printing job. He wanted to share it with me, giving me half, along with half of all future "gifts."

I wanted to ask how he could sink so low as to become such a disgusting turncoat. Instead, I remarked harshly that while he might have contacts in high places in the Communist party, I knew people in much higher places and might choose to expose him. My only reason for telling him that was for the satisfaction of making him worry.

I left without saying another word and never saw the man again. I went back to what had been my family's apartment to pick up my bundle and thank the daughter for allowing me to sleep in my own bed. But her father had walked in moments before I arrived. He told me that I was lucky not to be staying there. He held an important job in town, he said, allocating available coal for industrial and private use. Therefore he was allowed to have a gun and, sooner or later, he would have shot me. Angrily, I answered, "This is an important job, being drunk at home. I am not afraid of guns; the Germans did not shoot me. It was the opposite: I was shooting them. The best thing for you would be if you would shoot yourself."

My answer may have surprised him; he did not say a word. I knew I was being insulting, but by then I did not care. I was almost in shock, angry at the whole world. Perhaps if I had had a gun just then I would have gone on a shooting spree. I went directly to the "Joint" house, not wanting to see anything or talk to anyone in town. I stayed in Kalisz three days, a city where before the war lived 29,000 Jews, but where now there were almost none. Only about 350 survived, to scatter all over the world.

Later, when I was living in Germany, I inquired for a long time through the Red Cross or any other available organization about the fate of my family. The most accurate information I received was from a few survivors of the Warsaw ghetto who knew my family from my home town. They told me the details of how my family had been treated by the Germans: "evacuated" from home, everything confiscated, including the business. Western Poland had had to be "cleansed" — Aryanized — because it had been liberated and annexed, considered to be an integral part of the Greater German Reich. Those survivors told me of my family's life in the ghetto, with its poverty, fear, and anguish, and of their unthinkable final fate. One of the survivors, Stach Bierzwinski, even knew my extended family and could tell me about them. Their fate was the same as millions of others.

CHAPTER SEVEN

❧❧

Every day of the nearly six years of the war I dreamed of returning home, to reunite with my family and to resume the normal life we had had before. Now my dreams were shattered. I did not know what to do, with no family or friends to turn to for advice. I could not stay in town or even in the country which had contributed so much to my misery.

I heard from returning vagabonds that many people were traveling to Breslau to loot abandoned German apartments and other properties. Also, because of the war devastation, there were many opportunities for work. Without hesitation, I took the train to Breslau, for me a trip into the unknown. (Breslau in Silesia — in Polish, Wrocław na Śląsku — was historically a Polish town. After 1918 it was annexed to Germany. In 1945 it became Polish again.)

On the train I met a group of four people who had traveled the route many times, bringing loot with them every time. On their last trip they had carried many large bundles filled with dental supplies. They had found them in the rubble, stocked hidden in a basement. They were very proud of their discovery, telling me that on this trip alone they had made a fortune. They lived temporarily in a large apartment which belonged to a German widow. She took care of their rooms. Since they were officially registered as the inhabitants, the landlady was protected from having others moving in.

That was an important consideration, as German own-ers of large apartments were in fear of Russian soldiers or officers moving into their buildings. The Russians' drink-ing parties and orgies left the rooms in shambles, and, when after a short time they left, they took everything they could carry. The Russians' brawling could be heard throughout the neighborhoods all night: drinking, sing-ing, loud music — the screams of women being raped. Their motto was to get even for what the Germans had done to them.

With my credentials stating that I had recently been working in the graphic arts industry in Lithuania under the Communist administration, it was not difficult for me to find employment — especially since most of the people were busy looting and buying and selling on the black market instead of working.

One of the largest printing and offset-lithography com-panies in the city was named Brehmer & Minuth, located at 88 Matthiasstrasse. It had been heavily damaged in the fighting. Some walls were full of large holes from mortar fire. There was a large crater in the center of the court-yard through which a basement could be seen in which paper was stored. The plant was housed in a large three-story modern building with big windows — all of them broken. The machinery and other equipment was covered with all kinds of debris. It was a sad picture. My job was to put it back into operation.

As a reward I was given the keys to a large, furnished, abandoned apartment at 44 Matthias Street, plus some salary. The salary was barely sufficient to purchase any-thing from the black market. Anything at a reasonable price was sold in special stores for the Russians and party members only.

In the state of mind I was in, with no resources in a strange town, and faced with a task unlike any I had had before, I did not know where to begin. I was in the office, browsing through the files (after first having removed pieces of mortar from them and dusting them off), when I noticed a ledger with employee information. There was also information on the previous owners of the plant. Looking at an address I realized, to my surprise, that the apartment assigned to me had belonged to one of the former owners. He supposedly had run away to the West or another foreign country. (I had noticed an unusual amount of cut crystal in the apartment, even after someone had apparently helped himself to some of it).

I picked out addresses of some of the workers who lived within walking distance of the plant. The large city map on an office wall came in very handy. Since the only transportation I had available was my feet, I looked for the closest ones. At the first address I found an empty lot filled with rubble. The second house was boarded up. It had a warning sign on its front that indicated it was in dangerous condition with the possibility of collapse. I decided to try one more address that day.

Its front gate was locked. I rang the mechanical doorbell a few times. Finally a woman leaned out of a balcony and asked what I wanted. When I mentioned the name of the man I was looking for, she said that he was not at home and that she did not know where he was. I replied sadly that that was too bad, because I had an important message from his former employer, Brehmer & Minuth, which I had to give to him personally. When she heard that name, she told me to wait. I did, until I was ready to ring the bell again. Finally, another woman opened the gate. She introduced herself as the man's wife and asked for a message, as he was not at home. I told her that I had come, looking for help in locating essential employees so we could put the plant back into operation. She realized that if I had come in some official capacity I would have barged in without an explanation, perhaps even assisted by a militiaman. She politely and apologetically said that he might already have come home without her realizing it. I could wait while she checked. That made me angry. I told her that I did not need his help; I could ask someone else. I showed her my list.

For a German to be able to get an officially registered job during those months was a blessing. His apartment was protected from requisition; he himself was protected from being press-ganged into cleaning up the rubble from the destroyed buildings; and he was entitled to receive food coupons (without regard to how much food was available). When that woman realized that I was angry and ready to leave, she quickly opened the front gate and asked me to step in. Sure enough, the man I was looking for happened to be in their apartment.

I started by telling them that I did not like to be lied to. People who lied could not be trusted, or perhaps he was hiding because he had something on his conscience or a stain on his past. If he was not clean he had better tell me, because if I were to find out later—and I had ways of finding out—there would be consequences. They made many excuses, which I refused to listen to. The man told me all about himself: he had never done anything politically improper, and he never was a sympathizer with Nazism. (Strangely, after the war I never met a Nazi sympathizer. It made one wonder where all the Nazis and their sympathizers came from and where they disappeared to. In my view, if all the Nazi sympathizers had disappeared, there would have been few Germans left.) The former employee was very appreciative that I had contacted him, almost to the point of bowing and thanking me effusively. After their defeat many Germans were very good at this sort of performance.

The next morning three men showed up for work. We discussed their qualifications and their previous positions, which I compared against the ledger. I told them what their new responsibilities would be. We did not discuss wages because I did not know what the rates were. Also, I did not know where I would get the money to pay them or, for that matter, myself.

In any case, cash did not have much value at the time. The most important thing for them was to receive documents that certified they were officially employed in a government installation. They were also supposed to receive some food coupons. I issued temporary certificates, using the old company stamps.

Their first job was to clean up the bricks, mortar, dust, and other debris. After the bombardments and the fighting the place was a disaster. There was one bricked-up space in the basement that looked like some sort of bunker. However, there was a large hole smashed in the top and a ladder nearby. When I went to look inside I saw many empty cartons, some scattered clothing, and some broken glass dishes. The German employees told me that one of the previous owners had built the compartment to hide and protect his household goods, but the militia had "cleaned up" the area. There were two young armed militiamen always resting inside the gates of the plant, supposedly to protect the place from looting, but, obviously that law did not apply to them.

Other people learned about the plant, and I had a constant stream of people looking for jobs. Poles and Germans, craftsmen and pretenders, normal people, drunks, looters, and every other kind. One heavy German who looked like a wrestler came asking for a job as an auto mechanic. When I told him that we did not have any automobiles, he responded that he knew where one was hidden in a garage under the rubble. He offered to go with someone to the place. Curious about the mystery, I agreed to go with him. He worked for hours removing the bricks, sweating and grunting. I waited the whole time, also serving as protection to prevent anyone else from stealing the car. Finally, when he cleared a path and opened the stubborn gate, a nice Opel Cadet appeared. It had no outside damage, only being covered with dust. Someone must have purposely piled up the bricks to hide the garage. The car was not locked; the keys were in the ignition; and there was a full tank of gas. It started without difficulty. He wiped off the windshield and I said, "Let's go." We drove to the main militia station, where I registered the car as property of the printing plant—no questions asked. We drove the automobile to the plant, and the mechanic started working on it right away. He washed it first, so it looked spotless. I offered him a job as a chauffeur and plant mechanic. That was a fancy name for maintenance man.

I did not get to enjoy the car for long. I kept it in a shed in the courtyard of my apartment building. One afternoon when I returned from work, the caretaker excitedly told me that some Russian soldiers had lurched in, torn the padlock off the shed door, attached the car to their truck, and driven away. I immediately reported the incident to the militia, but they said it was a common occurrence. By now the soldiers might already be in Moscow or have sold the car for some vodka, they joked. In any case, the mechanic "found" another car, a larger one. I kept this one, an Opel Olympia, until I escaped to the West.

Gradually, with much effort and few outside resources, the plant began normal operations. French Premier Blum visited the city and came to our facilities. He was shown pictures of how it had looked after the war to compare against what had been accomplished. The next morning, on the front page of the local newspaper were articles about his visit, along with a photograph. The photo showed Premier Blum with me, described as "Dyrektor Państwowych Zakładow Graficznych No. 2" (Director of Federal Graphic Enterprise No. 2).

At the first anniversary "banquet" of the plant's operation I was praised by people from the Ministry of Education and Propaganda along with other dignitaries for our achievements. They applauded when, in my response, I gave all the credit to the workers.

But managing the plant was not easy. Several weeks later, two men from the Ministry's headquarters in Łódź arrived to check on operations. They were not craftsmen, only party members. After they learned of surplus money that was deposited in the bank, they were greatly surprised. They ordered me to immediately transfer the cash to their headquarters. I explained that the funds were intended for repairs and renovation of the apartment building at the front of the site. The building, part of which had been reduced to rubble, was supposed to be available for the employees who would be arriving from outside the city. To the surprise of everyone present, in no uncertain terms, they said that I had better do as I was told. Shortly afterwards I made the decision to leave Poland.

Joseph Stevens

I wanted to go to the United States, a country that my father had praised highly, but this was only wishful thinking. My father had spent four years in Denver, Colorado, when he had been in his twenties. After that time, he had visited the country a number of times, and each time on his return he told us about its wonders. Now I wanted to go there, but how could I? I had no resources or possible approaches, and I could not legally leave the country.

One day, Joe Fuchs arrived at my office. I knew him from before the war, as he had worked for a short time in my family's printing plant. He had somehow learned of my whereabouts. Joe lived in Łódź with his wife Gertrud, whom he had met in the village of Polichna where they spent the war years. He pretended to be an Aryan and worked there as a forester. She was Catholic, the wife of a physician who had been killed. They became close friends and married shortly after the war ended.

With them also lived his sister Mary. She had lived as an Aryan in Polichna during the war, pretending not to know her brother. She worked there, assisting the physician and helping the farmers' wives with chores.

Joe was planning to move to Breslau (Wrocław) because he had heard there were better opportunities. He and Mary had lost their entire family. I offered him temporary use of my apartment when they arrived after a few days. Some time later Mary and I became engaged.

All during this time I was working on plans to escape from Wrocław. Paradoxically, West Germany was my destination, as it was the closest country with official United States representation. While I could get a permit to travel to East Germany, then ruled by a Soviet-influenced Communist regime, it was impossible to negotiate its border with West Germany. Once, I even traveled to the eastern sector of Berlin, but one might as well have been in Russia.

We finally worked out plans to take a weekend "vacation" in the mountains, as I had previously with Mary. But this trip for all four of us was going to be permanent. We told no one of our plans for fear of prison, or worse. I obtained the address of a nice resort where I would meet the people who had the tickets we needed to proceed further. Carrying only small overnight bags and the keys to my apartment (which by then we had beautifully furnished and arranged), we were driven there by my chauffeur.

Once we arrived at the inn, I told my chauffeur that the surroundings were so nice I had decided to stay for a few more days. I gave him some money and told him to return by himself. I also gave him a short note to take to my assistant at the plant, excusing myself for a few days and giving him some instructions for while I was gone. I wanted my absence to appear genuine. I told the driver that I had found a vacancy in a nice large hotel at the nearby resort and would be moving there. That was the last time I saw him or, for that matter, anyone from the plant.

I already knew about the smuggling operation in the area. I made some contacts and obtained legal documents, including train tickets to Prague. In another pocket, though, were train tickets to Vienna, along with forged travel permits. I could not believe that things would happen the way they were supposed to. To my pleasant surprise, except for a few scary moments, the journey was uneventful. Of course, I did not feel safe until we had left the Russian Zone.

Once in Vienna we registered at an office for refugees

as displaced, stateless persons (DP's). From there we were sent to a DP camp in Puch, formerly an army camp. We lived in barracks, slept in wooden bunk beds with straw mattresses, and were fed as if we were in the army. But it felt like heaven knowing that we were free, even though we were not allowed to leave.

After a few months in Puch we were transported to another DP camp near Salzburg. It was much larger, but the conditions were almost the same. The scenery among the mountains was breathtaking, but it felt like being in a poor man's resort.

My only living uncle, Michael, lived in the United States. He had emigrated to Denver before the First World War, in 1912. I remembered discussions from home that mentioned a bank account at the National Colorado Bank in Denver. Uncle Mike was also supposed to have an account there. I wrote a letter to the bank, describing my situation and asking them if they might supply me with my uncle's address. I did not have access to any mailing facilities, so I asked an American GI who was guarding the camp. He promised to airmail the letter for me. Time passed, until I was losing hope that the letter had arrived at its destination or had even been mailed.

Finally, I received a long telegram from Uncle Mike, asking many questions, because he wanted to send me an affidavit, needed for emigration to the United States. I learned that the bank had received my letter, but, under the law, was not allowed to reveal customer addresses. Instead, they forwarded the letter to my uncle.

On the strength of the telegram we were allowed to leave the DP camp and move to Stuttgart, West Germany, in the American Zone. As DP's we registered at the police station and received an assignment to rent a room at 46

Bismarck Street. (Joe Fuchs and Gertrud got a different assignment.) We were also given ration cards, without which the only food available was from the black market. Stuttgart is also where Mary and I were married.

I received the affidavit from Uncle Mike through the Joint Distribution Committee. They were also helpful in making all the official arrangements for Mary and me to emigrate to the U.S. That same organization was very active in supporting needy DP's—and almost every DP was in some need.

The room that we rented was on the third floor of a house that belonged to an old German couple. The rental included the privilege of using all their facilities. Because of the severe housing shortage, families with larger living quarters were legally obliged to sublet parts of them. Mary started out on good terms with the landlady, Mrs. Leib, and we never did have a disagreement with them, even though we were sharing all the facilities. Mr. Leib was an old German grouch who was always complaining how badly Germany was being treated by the whole world. Mary often mentioned how she continued to exceed herself as she learned German cooking skills from Mrs. Leib. Dishes such as German soups, *Eintopfgericht* (stew), legumes, and others were even better later in the U.S. where food was abundant.

I never saw anyone visit the Leibs, not even any of their neighbors, except that, occasionally, a tall, broad-shouldered, well-built man would stop for very short visits. They spoke to each other in whispers. We considered it very thoughtful of them to not want to disturb us.

Occasionally, we exchanged greetings in passing with our neighbors in the hallway of the apartment house or on the steps. On the surface they seemed friendly enough, but we never really knew because we never developed any close acquaintances. They did know who we were, I assumed from the apartment manager, who originally had seen all our papers including the permit.

On one occasion as I passed an older neighbor, he asked me with a sarcastic smile, "How is the Leibs' son doing?" and mentioned his name. I was surprised and answered that I did not know that they had a son and had not met him. In a low voice the neighbor continued, wondering why I had never seen the one who sneaked in and out: the SS man. He mimed pointing to the place where the insignia was worn on the uniform, then held his hand high, indicating a high rank. He immediately excused himself and rushed down the steps. After what I had just heard sunk in, I wanted to ask him some questions; but by then he was already gone. When I entered my apartment I did not mention anything to Mary about what I had learned. It was too upsetting.

A few days later I happened to bump into Mr. Leib while no one else was around. We exchanged a few pleasantries. As we parted, I asked in a friendly voice, "And how is your son doing?" He seemed surprised at my question; it was the first time that either of us had referred to his son.

A few more weeks had passed when one afternoon Mrs. Leib knocked on the door of our room and invited us for tea. At that time tea was in short supply, so we expected some sort of herb tea; and herbs it was. Their son sat at the table, introduced as "our son, the engineer, who is so busy with his work that he doesn't even have time to visit his parents." We started talking about banal things. The son told us how busy he was in some machine factory, which was badly damaged during the war. I replied that conditions were very hard now and they must have been very hard during the war. He admitted that they were, his tone expecting some sympathetic words. But instead, I said that it was very, very hard on my family and myself, too. Only by a miracle was I still alive. I could have been murdered, along with the millions of other Jews, by the Germans. At that moment Mary kicked me, hard, under the table.

Mr. and Mrs. Leib were also surprised because in our previous discussions on the subject they had claimed complete ignorance and sorrow, an attitude I found typical of Germans. Now the son excitedly claimed that there might have been some cases like that in the East, but the executions were performed by the Ukrainians, Lithuanians, Poles, and others, not by the Germans. Mary insisted that we change the subject, but I was no longer calm. Looking him straight in the eye, I demanded to know why, some time after the annexation of the eastern territories to Germany proper, all the German press had boasted that those territories were *Judenfrei* (free of Jews)? "Where had those hundreds of thousands of Jews gone and who got rid of them?" I asked. "Why, in the largest concentration camp, where my family had been taken to die, was the sign *"Arbeit macht frei"* ("Work makes you free") in German? And why was this camp—actually a murder factory, with its gas chambers, crematoria, gallows, and other equipment of death—operated exclusively by Germans, with members of the elite SS making the decision to send a person directly to the gas chambers or to wait under inhuman conditions to die? All Europe knew about it, and here nobody knows how people were sent to heaven. Where are the missing millions? You know there are thousands of photographs in existence of the executions. These pictures were made by Germans of Germans doing these deeds. The photographs are of Germans in the uniforms of their special units, made by official German photographers and others showing Germans smiling, happy, proud while killing the Jews in the most brutal ways. The German population didn't know anything about it, including you? You who were in a position in one of the most prestigious Nazi organization?"

No one said a word after I had finished. Mary, very upset, got up, thanked them for the tea, and we left the room. For a while our relations with the Leibs were very cool, and we hardly talked to each other. They never mentioned our discussion and never challenged anything I said at the tea. Then things returned to normal. The Leibs became very amiable and kind, at least on the surface. We never saw their son again, and I never asked about him. In any case, I started work soon after that and Mary was the one who mostly dealt with them.

I heard similar things from other Germans. They pretended to know nothing about what had happened during the war. Hadn't they read the newspapers or listened to the radio? Didn't they have relatives who returned on furloughs from the conquered territories? And what about themselves? There weren't too many Germans who had not served in some kind of military unit outside Germany. Sometimes at work I overheard conversations among the employees of Schreiber Verlag. They had served in the German armed forces in the conquered territories. They discussed openly, even with some pride, the goods they had shipped home or brought with them while they were serving in the East. I always asked myself, didn't they realize that the items, some very valuable, previously belonged to someone who had been murdered?

Good Morning

All the DP's in town were living in a camp or in private apartments. Though they were supported by the "Joint," most of them supplemented their incomes by trading on the black market, which was thriving. Not having talent in that field, I did not participate. Instead, I investigated what was going on in my trade and profession.

Near Stuttgart, in Nellingen by Neckar (a river), was the oldest publishing and printing house of children's color books: Schreiber Verlag. Not having suffered any war damage, they were operating at full production. Paper, which was very scarce everywhere else, was abundant in their storerooms. I visited them and asked for a job. I was immediately accepted, due to the shortage of craftsmen. They said that many of their employees had disappeared in the war. As I later learned, I was the only Jew working immediately after the war in a German enterprise.

I commuted to work on a fast electric train. From Stuttgart to Esslingen-Nellingen station took twenty minutes. The ride was nice, and the scenery was pleasant. During the harvest season I could see people picking grapes. They looked very small in the distance against a background of terraced hills.

We ate lunch at a nearby bierstube. The waitress always brought each of us, without asking, a mug of locally brewed beer. She then told us what was available and cut points out of our ration cards after we ordered. During lunch we talked about almost everything: work, world events, the economy, politics. Mostly, the other workers complained of how poorly and unjustly the rest of the world treated the Germans. I told them why a few times, but most of the time I kept quiet, knowing that they knew full well. It was fashionable for Germans to complain and blame the Allies.

Joseph Stevens

At work I became close to the head of the reproduction department, Karl Hirsch, and his son, Willy. We improved some standard procedures and developed a photographic emulsion used for lithography. It could be successfully etched when coated onto a glass photographic plate (plastic film bases for lithography had not yet been developed).

I also developed an automatic container for storing and dispensing lithographic emulsion. Coating a glass plate with emulsion had to be done in total darkness because the panchromatic emulsion was sensitive to any color of light. The apparatus needed only one hand to operate, while the other was used to support a glass plate perfectly level. (The plate could be up to thirty by forty inches and had to be supported on the tips of one's fingers.) As air conditioning was not available, water had to be used for temperature control. It was run through a thin-walled copper coil hidden inside the unit. Finally, two buttons operated opposing springs, opening and closing the doors that ran on tracks in the cylindrical device. I applied for and received a Patent Pending certificate. (When I came to the United States I brought with me both the certificate and the heavy device. I soon learned that it was obsolete, because precoated dry plates were available from several manufacturers.)

At one point I was asked to produce and print some books for the U.S. Armed Forces. They were bilingual dictionaries for the foreign troops who were serving under U.S. command. The U.S. military provided us with good quality printing paper which had been insulated and crated for its voyage from America. The crates were of such fine quality that the wood could have been used for building furniture. The Germans argued over who would get to keep it. The books themselves bore two imprints on the front page: "Property of United States Government" and "Reproduction by Joseph Szczecinski." I still have one of them.

I worked at Schreiber Verlag for two anxious years, waiting my turn to receive an immigration visa to America. I was luckier than some, who had been waiting for four years for an opening in their country's quota. But if I had been born in Russia I would have received the visa right away. Before the war Russians had not been allowed to emigrate to the United States. It was considered treason. Therefore, the Russian quota had plenty of places available.

Finally, after almost three long years of waiting, I received the wonderful message that I had gotten the visa. I immediately quit my job. I also purchased a large process camera. It was about ten feet tall and was considered state-of-the-art. It was difficult to obtain from the factory without some preferential treatment. Therefore, I asked Karl Hirsch for assistance. The camera was specially crated for overseas shipment.

When I finally received a notice from an American government agency for an interview, I knew that my trip was near. I think the agency was the CIA. On average, people spent about ten minutes in this kind of interview. I was grilled for about an hour, despite being able to speak in German with them. I assumed that something must have been wrong, but I could not figure out what it was. The only thing I could think of was that they had learned of my army activities, which I had left out of my curriculum vitae. (On the other hand, the subject never came up in the questioning.) I had been advised by some "experts" that the less complicated my history, the better, especially my involvement in armed struggle. I could not document what army it was, my position, or activities. At the time, I could not obtain any witnesses or affidavits.

Finally, I was told that my interview was okay and that I was clear to emigrate to the United States. I was so curious that I could not help asking politely if the unusual length of the interview meant that they had found something wrong with me. I was told that everything I reported in my application had been supported by a document or a notarized copy. During the postwar period, when so many documents and files had been destroyed or lost, people truthfully claimed that they were unable to find them. My case looked suspicious because nothing had been left undocumented. Were they real or falsified? Also, it seemed questionable that I worked at a private German firm for peanuts. After seeing the surprised and worried look on my face, one official reassured me that everything was now fine.

Before receiving the visa, though, I had to pass one more obstacle: the final interview at the consulate. I stepped into the handsome office with its large, beautifully ornamented mahogany desk and leather armchair only to see, as my first impression, an important American official with his feet on the desk. The official told me to sit down. After a few routine questions, he asked, "When you become an American citizen, which party will you vote for in the elections? For the Democrats, Republicans, or some other?"

I was floored. Was the official a Republican, Democrat, or what? Was this a trap or just a routine question? After a silence, I finally answered, "I am really not yet acquainted with the exact programs of the political parties. One thing I know for sure is that whatever party I vote for will be okay, because I imagine that all the political parties in the United States are based on the principle of democracy."

The official burst out laughing and said that once I was in the United States I would learn otherwise. When I listened to Republicans I would hear only bad things about the Democrats, and the other way around. I was quite embarrassed to hear him saying that sort of thing and did not know why he brought it up. But, never having moved from his lounging position, he congratulated me and wished me good luck in the United States.

When I left that office, I finally felt that, at last, I could be sure that I was going to the United States.

We left Stuttgart by train, heading for Hamburg. There, we boarded one of the Liberty boats, the *Ernie Pyle*. The trip took eight long days during stormy weather. The ship was tossed about like a matchbox. The noise of the engines and of the waves hitting the sides made it seem that the ship would break up at any minute. Most of the passengers became seasick, starting on the second day of the voyage. I had never been to sea and spent most of the voyage on the deck, where the salt spray and the cold wind kept me refreshed. Mary, however, spent most of the time in one of the women's cabins. I was able to visit her only twice. All she ate for the entire voyage were a few American Red Delicious apples. Finally, on March 21, 1949, we arrived in New York. Mary was very weak and drawn.

We were greeted with flowers in New York by our friends, the Roliders. They had arrived in America three years earlier. Once our papers were processed, we had intended to proceed by train to Detroit, where my Uncle Mike now lived. But to our disappointment, Henry Rolider had arranged for us to delay our trip. All our baggage, however, did go to Detroit; and, after a big dispute with the customs authorities, the large crate with the process camera was also shipped.

I had all the bills and documents allowing me to take the camera with me to the United States, but the customs agent still insisted that I open the crate so he could check the contents. I had no tools with me, so I had one of the porters unscrew two of the boards for inspection. It took him a long time to remove, and later replace, the thick boards. I realized that the crate was built like a tank, with inside reinforcements, for overseas shipping. The whole thing was so heavy that four longshoremen were needed to move it. I was charged an exorbitant sum for their services which, fortunately, I was able to borrow from Henry Rolider.

We finally arrived at the Roliders' luxurious Manhattan apartment completely exhausted. Even the spacious, beautifully arranged room they provided did not impress us. But they wanted to show us a good time. I called Uncle Mike and let him know what had happened. He agreed to arrange for storing our luggage and asked us to let him know, the next day, when we would arrive. But day after day I called Detroit, further postponing our arrival. Finally, after six exhausting days and nights in New York, not sleeping before 2:00 a.m., we couldn't stand the pace anymore. We thanked the Roliders for their hospitality, and I called Uncle Mike to let him know we would be arriving the next day. We would be waving white sheets of paper at the train station for him to recognize us.

He saw us as soon as we stepped off the train. After a warm and emotional welcome, we rode home in his big Oldsmobile 99. After the small cars I had driven in Europe the Oldsmobile seemed like a bus. He took us to his beautiful, large house on Ohio Avenue, then one of

Good Morning

Detroit's more affluent neighborhoods. Once we arrived, Aunt Fannie showed us to "our" room. It was actually my cousin Regina's room; but since she had been working for many years in Alaska as a government social worker, the room was unused. The house and its atmosphere made us feel as if we had arrived in heaven. The next day we went to the train depot to retrieve our luggage, which had been waiting for us for a week. The process camera in its crate we placed in storage.

Uncle Mike took me for a ride around Detroit to show me the town. As we turned from Grand Boulevard onto East Milwaukee Avenue, I noticed a large sign: "National Lithographic Co." I asked Uncle Mike if we might stop there to see what was going on. Once inside the plant he explained that I hoped I would be able to see the plant. Instead, we were ushered into the president's office. Jack Moore, Sr., who was also the owner, received us warmly. With Uncle Mike serving as interpreter, he asked me all about myself. Then, without me even asking, he offered me a job and said that I could start work the next day. I was so surprised by the offer that I did not know what to say. At first I just thanked him and continued on. Uncle Mike hesitated, but finally, with Jack Moore looking at him, he translated, "I am eventually planning to start my own business, but I assure you that I will in no way be a competitor."

Later, Uncle Mike told me what Jack must have thought, hearing the assurances of someone who had just stepped off the boat, could not speak English, and had no experience in the United States, assuring the owner of the largest lithographic plant in Detroit (it had 220 employees), that he would not compete with him. But I had dreamed of having my own plant in the United States. I simply wanted to be honest with my future employer, who seemed like a very nice guy.

The next day I went to work. Uncle Mike, not wanting me to get lost, wrote out addresses and showed me the bus stops where I had to get on, get off, and transfer. I remembered the place where I had to transfer: on the overpass across from the General Motors Building on Grand Boulevard. My stop to get off for home was near a large billboard with a Marlboro advertisement. I tried to memorize all the landmarks.

Everything worked fine, except that I missed my stop on the way home. I reached the last stop and noticed that I was the only passenger left. I showed the address to the driver, and he told me that I had missed the stop. I held my hands out to the side, pantomiming, "where?" The driver understood, believing that I was either mute or could not speak English. He motioned to me to sit down and wait. On his way back he would tell me where I should get off. When I stepped off the bus, I looked for the Marlboro billboard that was my landmark. It had been replaced with another during the day!

On my first day of work I took the white lab coat I had worn in Germany with me. I was the only one who wore a white coat. People started calling me "Doc." Otherwise, they called me by my first name because they could not pronounce "Szczecinski."

When I received my first paycheck, I was so surprised by its size that I went to the office to report the mistake. They checked and told me that it was okay; the pay rate had been set by Mr. Moore. They also told me, however, that I was the first person who had ever felt he was receiving too large a check.

Living in the United States it was a problem that no

one could spell or pronounce my last name. Michigan had a legal requirement of one year's residency before someone could go to court to change his name. One year and one day after I arrived, I was in court. The bailiff announced the case: "Mr. and Mrs. Joseph..." He stopped for a while, then spelled out, "S-z-c-z-e-c-i-n-s-k-i." Normally the judge asked why someone wanted to change his name, but, smiling, he said that it was not necessary this time. Back at work, I went to the office to tell them that I had changed my name to one that was easy to spell: Stevens. I was shocked when they asked if it was spelled with a "ph" or a "v." I had acquired a new problem!

One evening I received a telephone call from Chicago. The caller had a heavy German accent and introduced himself as the U.S. representative of and distributor for the Hunt Chemical Company of Germany. I asked him to speak German so that we could communicate better. I was surprised that he knew as much about me as if we had known each other for a long time. Curious, I asked from where he knew me. He replied that Karl Hirsch, my friend at Schreiber Verlag, had recommended me. He continued, saying that he had a wonderful offer to present me, but that I would have to meet him in his office in Chicago. I could not resist the mystery and made an appointment for an upcoming weekend. I had an idea that he might have wanted to start a new business, because I had told Karl in Stuttgart that I wanted to do so when I reached America. I had already started planning it.

When I reached the representative's office, he came right to the point: Hunt Chemical wanted me to be their technical representative in South America! That was easy; I rejected the offer on the spot. I pointed out, in German, that I knew no Spanish and my English would make it hard to communicate. He spoke persuasively, telling me language would not be a problem, that I would have an assistant who would speak with me in German. Still, I thanked him. Perhaps some time in the future . . .

I did not accept his offer to repay my travel expenses and took my leave, not sorry that I had rejected the job. We had not even settled in Detroit. To move again to start life in an unknown country was unthinkable.

On my way home in the train I found that I was not angry to have wasted the day. On the contrary, I was happy to have been in Chicago for the first time. Even more, I was pleased to learn that other opportunities were opening for me. For the first time since I had arrived in the United States my ego grew and I kept my head up.

Back in Detroit, I had been in National's color reproduction department for more than two months when I was called into Jack Moore's office. I thought that something must have been wrong. Jack asked me about my job, how I liked it, and so on. I had the opportunity to thank him for starting me at such a high wage. He replied that it was the first time he had hired a new employee without being asked how much he would be receiving. Also, after hearing about my experience in the profession, he would have been embarrassed to give me the starting rate. He did not regret his decision—in fact, from now I would be earning even more.

I did not understand much of what he was telling me, guessing at what he said, but unwilling to admit that I did not understand it. I did learn why he called me into his office. The foreman in the color reproduction department was quitting to start a business with two other employees. Jack asked me to take over, explaining my new responsibilities and the pay raise. Still not believing I understood him correctly, I sat without speaking, confused. I said something about communication and my English. He waved his hand and said, "Baloney!" That was another new word I did not understand, so I remained still. He took my silence to be acceptance of his offer.

The following day I reported to work together with the outgoing foreman. We became close friends. I helped him organize his new plant (Tri Litho, after three partners) and consulted again later when it was in production.

Everything was progressing more smoothly than I had expected. The only thing that bothered me early on was when people failed at some project or task and used the excuse, "I couldn't understand Joe." From then on, when explaining something to someone, I took hold of one of his coat buttons and did not let go until that person repeated the instructions back to me. That changed my nickname from "Doc" to "Joe with the button."

I could not stand the condition of the equipment, so I started making changes. I took care to make changes in the most economical way and to explain what I was doing and why. In return, management was supportive and cooperative, never refusing my requests.

One weekend, with only a guard working in the plant, I brought the tools and supplies I needed to clean and scrape the glossy paint from the 16-foot horizontal process camera. I then repainted it with matte black enamel to look like new. I was even proud of it. Monday morning, no one, except for my management, knew who had done the work.

The next weekend I painted the light-trap entrance and the walls of the main darkroom with glossy yellow-orange enamel, much like the color of Kodak film packages. It was an unusual color for a darkroom; in the U.S. they were painted very dark green or flat black, in the theory that if a ray of light would strike a wall, the paint would absorb it rather than reflect it onto the light-sensitive photographic plates. My own thinking was that by making the darkroom light-tight, no stray light would enter in the first place. Therefore, the color of the walls wouldn't matter. Besides, the light-colored darkroom might be kept cleaner, as any dirt could be seen. Also, people would feel better working in "sunshine" than in a dungeon.

I found that I had a lot to learn in a new country. One evening I unexpectedly had to work late. The phone rang and rang without being answered. Finally, I lifted the receiver and bravely said, "Hello." The president of the company immediately replied, "Joe, what are you doing in the plant at this time of day?" He had been able to recognize me out of all the employees from a single word. It made me realize how heavy my accent was.

But I had some satisfaction, too. The first year I worked at National, Jack Moore decided to go, along with two other executives, to the Industrial Graphic Show and Convention in Windsor, Ontario. He invited me, too. Not yet having U.S. citizenship or a passport, I had to quickly arrange for a travel permit. On our return trip, at the border checkpoint, the border official asked each of the others where they had been born. But he took one look at me, said thank you, and let me go. I joked that I must have been the only one who looked American. They didn't forgive me for that for a long time.

One accomplishment gave my career at National another boost. The company had been requested to submit a bid to United Airlines for a series of forty large full-color travel posters, to be delivered in a very short time. Key personnel met to establish a strategy to produce the posters by the deadline should the company be awarded the order. Because of the time constraint, the decision was made to print the posters at National but to farm out the reproductions (up to and including the offset plate-making) of thirty of the forty.

For some reason that did not sit well with me; perhaps my ambitions were frustrated. After some figuring, I interrupted, saying that it was not necessary to send out | anything. We could reproduce all of the posters more economically and more quickly in our own plant. Jack Moore asked, "Are you sure? This is an important project for National, and we are responsible for our commitment."

I did not say a word, only nodded. Then, realizing what I was gambling, I froze for a moment. I told the meeting that retouching would be unnecessary, and the work of the dot etchers would be cut in half. I, myself, would do one similar reproduction with one assistant and would have the set of color separations ready by the next morning for evaluation. That was my insurance: I could back out in the morning if everything did not come out right.

We worked all night. The method I was using, photomechanical silver masking, was one I had used in Europe, but it was not yet common in the United States. (I had explained it and proposed it previously at National, but the retouching department would not accept it, knowing that some of them would lose their jobs.) I wasted a lot of expensive materials in experimentation. I was pooped the next morning as I displayed the work for evaluation, but fortunately, everything turned out as I had predicted. We agreed to proceed.

After the meeting, Jack Moore clapped me on the shoulder and said, "Good job, Joe." On the basis of its revised estimate, National was awarded the entire project. I completed my part of the job even more quickly than I had projected, leaving more time for the printing.

Some time later, representatives from Eastman Kodak demonstrated their newly patented Kodak magenta masking system. They got good results, but it took them five hours. I asked if they could stay for one more hour, so I could show them how my procedure worked. After an hour of fast work with my assistant I laid my set of glass plates on a light table next to theirs and invited them to compare the two. The results were so obvious that they did not make any more effort to sell us Kodak's new system.

After a few weeks I received an invitation to visit Eastman Kodak's research laboratories in Rochester, New York. It was unusual, as they were generally off-limits to outsiders. My company insisted that I accept the invitation. They even agreed to pay for my time away and for my travel expenses.

My first surprise was to see the walls in all their darkrooms painted gray. I learned that Kodak had just repainted them from black. My hosts told me that they were familiar with the idea I had presented to them in Detroit, and, after much experimentation, their chemists had chosen neutral gray, which later became the standard for the industry. That was the end of the "sunshine" which National's workers had liked so much.

As we continued on to the laboratories, I noticed that the signs outside rooms were made of frosted glass painted with black letters and lit from behind with incandescent bulbs. The uneven lighting made them almost unreadable, much like the cabin signs on old airplanes. I suggested that they replace the matte glass with white opal (translucent) glass to create a more even illumination. This small suggestion made me a celebrity there.

From that time on I was often invited to learn about new technologies, but I also made it a point to bring with me some suggestion. I passed them along to the Doctor of Chemistry who was in charge of their lab department. I was told that he was putting my ideas into the company suggestion box under his name. To make it legal, he was paying me a dime for each suggestion. Other people from the lab began greeting me, jokingly, with the question of what I had for sale that day for the manager. I enjoyed doing it, and we became close friends. Sadly, he died of a heart attack at a young age.

I also developed a very good relationship with the Photo Products Division of the DuPont Company after their representative, Ray Hushebeck, found out about my visits to Rochester. He was a very nice person, elegant and good-looking. On his visits to Detroit and, later, to Grand Rapids, Mary and I enjoyed going out with him for the evening. He hadn't had many years of experience in the industry and, therefore, liked discussing different areas with me.

One time, Ray showed me, in confidence, what looked like a quarter-inch-thick piece of plastic. He explained that it could be rolled to seven one-thousandths of an inch thick, or four thousandths, or even thinner, and still be indestructible. It was called Mylar. It would replace all the other materials used as the base of photographic films, in particular the old acetate material, which was brittle and flammable, even explosive. Mylar was none of these.

DuPont enlisted National, represented by me, as one of the pilot plants entrusted to use and experiment with the new product before it was finally released on the market. I agreed to report to its lab, in Wilmington, Delaware, what I learned about its good and bad features.

Mylar's best feature was that it was dimensionally stable. With none of today's modern film processing machinery available, film wet from processing had to be dried like laundry on a clothesline, sometimes with help from a fan. Large pieces even had to be squeegeed before drying. Instead of tediously squeegeeing the water from a 30-by-40-inch sheet of film, I found that I could crack it like a whip to remove the water without kinking it. It even sounded like a whip. Ray Hushebeck was impressed enough with my demonstration that, when the film was finally introduced to the market, he asked me to repeat it in front of others.

By 1956 I felt it was time to open my own plant, but I didn't know where. It couldn't be in Detroit, as I had made a commitment to Jack Moore when he hired me. I wanted to learn where there might be good opportunities for future growth, so I took advantage of my relationship with Eastman Kodak and visited their director of planning in Rochester. After I had explained the reason for my visit, he was resistant, concerned for the confidentiality of their files and the precedent of offering private advice. I pointed out that I was not interested in the files — in fact, I had provided Kodak with not a little information for their files, gratis. I only wanted his advice. Finally, he relented, and revealed that good areas to consider were Colorado and California.

I also made an appointment to visit the general director of the National Lithographers Association, whom I also knew personally. The Association was the most prestigious organization in our industry, the sixth largest in the United States. I flew directly from Rochester to New York to meet with him. He, too, advised me to consider Colorado and California. I had been hoping to hear something different, though. I did not want to move so far again to another completely unfamiliar area.

But, in our conversation, the director told me a story that continued to guide me: A rich man started a large, fancy restaurant at one corner of a particular intersection in a town. A year later, he went broke. At the same time, on the opposite corner of the same intersection, a poor man started a very small restaurant. He put in continual effort to improve it. After a year it had become a large, elegant restaurant whose business kept growing. The point was that the location of a business is much less important than how it is managed.

Back in Detroit, the manager of the Dickinson lithographic plant of Grand Rapids was visiting town. I had known him when he was managing Cadillac Printing in Detroit. His advice was to start anywhere in Western Michigan, which lacked a high-quality color reproduction facility. He, in fact, had to use firms in Chicago, Milwaukee, and Cincinnati.

That led me to investigate Grand Rapids. At the time, the city was the national center of the furniture industry, which was always looking for quality reproduction for their marketing and advertising materials.

I made an appointment to meet with Jack Moore. I told him that the time of my dreams was now ripe and that I was planning to start my own business in Grand Rapids. He tried to talk me out of it, emphasizing the hardships, competitiveness, financial risk, and other negative aspects of starting a business compared to working for him. I told him that I had made up my mind, realizing that it was a big gamble. I reminded him that I had been honest in telling him of my plans when he had offered me a job. (Jack said that he remembered it but had taken it as a joke.) I also reminded him how grateful I had been when, during a strike by the union, he called me at home, telling me to keep it a secret that I would be getting a paycheck in the mail for the duration of the strike. I was receiving two checks: one from the company and the other from the union as strike benefits. (I later realized that he had done it because he did not want me looking for another job, knowing that I had already rejected some offers.)

I asked Jack how much longer I should stay, to give him time to find a replacement. He asked me to make it my responsibility to find a replacement and to stay until then.

In the meantime, I started looking for equipment for a new plant. It was easier than I had thought. One of the largest suppliers in the United States, Doughitt Corporation, located in Detroit, offered me unlimited credit. One device I ordered was a special double-sided, transparent, rotating vacuum frame, 50-by-60-inches, which I had designed. It had many features not available in other frames on the market. Most importantly, it could double productivity. Doughitt offered to build it for me for free if they could make it a standard model in their catalog. I purchased a used horizontal 20-by-24-inch process camera, for which I bought extra sets of lenses and built adapters, to enable it to produce 30-by-40-inch and larger images. This amazed even the people at Doughitt. I made a deal for materials with Garrick Photo Supply in Detroit. Finally, I convinced DuPont to supply me with Mylar film stock, still not on the market, as long as I did not tell anyone what it was or where it came from.

I was all set. So, on Memorial Day in 1956, I set out in my brown 1953 Ford to find a place in Grand Rapids. My only acquaintance there was out of town. For that matter, it looked as if everyone was out of town. There was no traffic, and nobody was out on the streets. The city looked like a ghost town. No restaurants were open. I was told that I might find one open in the Pantlind Hotel; but by the time I got there, it was closed, too. By that time, very hungry, I spotted a man on the street who referred me to a bar in Wyoming, Michigan, on the corner of South Division and 28th Street. Driving along South Division, I spotted a large sign in a long window: "5,000 sq. ft.—air conditioned, for lease." I stopped and peered through the dirty glass window. It looked fine: a large open area that I was already starting to lay out in my mind. I called the telephone number listed in the window, but, of course, no one answered.

Back in Detroit, the next day, I called the number and made an appointment for the following Saturday. The agent, a Mr. Cassis, had his office just across the street from the building above Hattems Restaurant. He showed me through the place, including the basement. When we returned to his office, we discussed terms. I could sign a five-year lease at one exorbitant rate or a two-year lease at an even higher rate. A security deposit equivalent to three month's rent was also required.

I explained my situation, pointing out that my business might not even last for two years. He looked down, happening to notice the Masonic ring on my finger. After we had exchanged some personal information, he changed his tune. The building, at 411 South Division, belonged to the Ellis family. It had been a popular Grand Rapids nightclub, The Town Pump, managed by a family member named Fusie, but it had been vacant for more than two years.

He asked me how much rent I could afford. I replied,

$300 monthly, but when the business took off I would be able to pay more. Surprisingly, he agreed. He went on to say that no deposit or lease would be required and the first month would be free, for renovation. The building had been vacant for so long, he explained, that the Ellises had given him a free hand. Besides, he added, they had plenty of money. We shook hands, and that was it. I did insist on getting something in writing with the monthly rate and the due date of the first payment. Some time later, I signed a formal one-year lease. Mr. Cassis remained very helpful in locating responsible electricians, carpenters, plumbers, and painters.

Despite the good deals I was making, starting a new business took a lot of money. I had been building our savings in a number of ways. I realized that the process camera I had dragged with me from Germany was not the right kind for the business I was going into. Therefore, I sold it to the Aaronson Company, a printing firm in Detroit, as the ideal instrument for their fast production needs.

Every week, when I cashed my paycheck, I allotted a small amount for living expenses, sent some to Joe and Gertrud Fuchs in Stuttgart, and placed the rest in a savings account. (After a while, she wrote to me asking not to send them any more money, because Joe was losing it playing the horses. So, without him knowing, I mailed small amounts every few weeks directly to her.)

Uncle Mike was always preaching to me never to play the stock market. It was too much of a gamble for a novice like myself. I learned that he had lost everything in the 1929 crash. His integrity had kept him from declaring bankruptcy, and he had spent years repaying his debts, never recovering his financial position before the crash. But the stock market fascinated me. As a result, I did something that I never told him—the only secret I kept from Uncle Mike.

From money I set aside for the purpose, I bought two shares of IBM stock. When it went up I sold it, making a profit. I kept this money separate from my other savings and continued to add small amounts to it each week. When I had enough, I purchased five shares of IBM stock. (I bought IBM because the company interested me. I read everything I could about it.) I sold the five shares, again at a profit, and felt like a tycoon. I kept saving and buying, putting each block of twenty shares into a safe deposit box at Michigan National Bank. From my modest savings, the rise in the stock, its dividends and splits, I accumulated enough shares of IBM stock to pay for starting my business. We were able to use our regular savings account later to make a down payment on our house.

At National, in Detroit, I recommended a replacement and worked together with him for three weeks. Jack Moore assured me that the door would always be open for me and that I could return any time. This made me feel good and gave me a sense of security.

I named my new company National Correct Color Service: "National" after my employer in Detroit, and "Correct" to describe the quality of the work. I drew up plans for the new plant in Grand Rapids, including the positions of all the equipment and other details. I also marked the walls, floor, and ceiling for locations of electrical outlets, faucets, drain pipes, and other fixtures. As a result, everything went in without changes, to the disappointment of the workmen. They made their greatest profit on changes. I tried to be there to help whenever I could. The toughest job was when I rented a wallpaper steamer and tried to remove the washable wallpaper. Standing on a tall ladder, I sweated more than the steamer itself.

Early every morning I drove three hours from Detroit to work with the tradesmen, and each evening I returned home. The I-96 expressway had not been built at that time, so I had to drive on two-lane roads through Lansing, East Lansing, and all the small towns along the way. After two weeks of this I decided to stay in town during the work-week. I took a room at the Grand Rapids Motel, two miles south of the city on South Division. The clean air was re-freshing when I was awakened each dawn by the crow-ing of the rooster on the adjacent farm.

When everything was ready for production I went to say my final good-byes at National and offered assistance whenever they might need it. (They took advantage of it first thing the following week when they had difficulty producing a color catalog for General Electric. I immedi-ately drove to Detroit and spent a half-day with my re-placement.) As I was leaving, they told me that they would not let me off the hook that easily. They handed me my first order: a small color catalog needed for fast delivery. When I returned to deliver it in person they gave me a bigger one. But I still needed skilled people, who were not available in Grand Rapids. The people I hired had to be trained or retrained.

At this time, also, I moved my family to Grand Rapids. It was difficult to find a house to rent. Finally we found a temporary place, on Elmwood N.E., a house owned by the wife of a well-known lawyer. The "temporary" rental lasted three years, until we bought our house on Sligh Boulevard.

I called Random House publishers in New York. I had been making color covers for their paperback editions when I worked in Germany. I informed them that I had started my own plant in Grand Rapids. They asked, "Where?" After I explained that Grand Rapids was in Michigan, their second question was, "Why Grand Rapids?" I told them that I would explain it to them when I was in New York. I was lucky that they did not ask how large the plant was. After that, I was so busy with their work that I could not accept any others' orders.

I made my business cards out of DuPont's Cronar material, similar to Mylar. DuPont liked the idea and later printed their own cards on the same plastic. My cards were folded in half; the second page was printed with the words, "Business Notes." Any writing could be easily erased later. The greatest attraction of the cards was my standing offer of one hundred dollars to anyone who was able to tear one. I had to replace a lot of mutilated ones, because people tried all sorts of ways to tear them, but I never had to shell out the hundred dollars.

I hired more people, keeping in mind what my father once said to me: "I cannot produce much by myself. But if I hire one person and, on his performance, profit one dollar a day, I can hire ten people and make ten dollars a day." In later years, at the peak, we employed forty-two people. Because of the reputation we built, we never had to hire a salesperson to solicit business.

One of the people I hired was from South Bend, Indiana. I gave him the fancy title of Technical Representative. I needed him to be our line of communication to out-of-state customers, like RCA, Eli Lilly, and Studebaker. I trained him in communication skills by taking him on my visits to local customers, including Gerber, Upjohn, Whirlpool, and Gibson. I even gave him a small tape recorder to tape the customers' orders for complex projects (with their permission). He worked out well enough that I hired another person from Detroit to cover other distant accounts.

We outgrew our old plant and needed to expand. When building the new US-131 expressway, the city had torn down houses along part of its path and rezoned the resulting vacant lots for light industrial use. We bought one of the lots, along Scribner NW. We also purchased a nearby lot from the state, property surplus from the building of the expressway. No one wanted it because of its odd, triangular shape. We wanted it for parking in case we had to expand our plant into part of our parking lot. Later, though, the city bought it back for parking at the newly constructed Grand River Fish Ladder.

Those were the happy years. Even times of very hard work were balanced by the satisfaction of achievement. Morale in the plant was high. Some employees developed a motto: "If someone else can't do it, we will. If others can do it, we will do it better. If we don't know how to do it, Joe will do it."

One of our innovations was to place communications units at everyone's station. They were surplus remote jukebox units (the type that used to be common in restaurant booths) that had been rewired to serve as intercoms, public address units, and background music speakers. Everyone could adjust his volume or simply shut it off.

As in any business, along with the good times were some bad ones. The worst ones for me happened because of my business inexperience and naïveté. I took two partners who, after more than twenty years, forced me out of the company. Encouraged by many customers and friends, I decided to start another business, this time without partners. My biggest and most important customers, in particular, wanted to transfer all their work to my new plant, saying that people with such dirty and unethical business practices could not be trusted.

I found a vacant building on the west side of Grand Rapids and started to draw up plans. This would be a state-of-the-art plant, a showcase of the industry. But Mary, concerned about the level of stress I was under, rejected the idea of my starting a new business. She did not want to see me, now in my fifties, go through the same hardships I had in my thirties.

Then I received an opportune call from a vice president at Amway Corporation inviting me to a business lunch. There, he said, "Joe, now that you don't have any responsibilities any more, why don't you join Amway? You could assist us by streamlining some problems which you are well aware of."

My business relationship with Amway had begun not long after the founders started the business. At that time they had about 100 employees in their plant. I accepted the position for one year. After that year, I was asked to stay another year, then another and another, until, after seven years, I decided to retire at the age of 67.

Even then, I was approached by several companies that asked me for technical advice and problem solving. Whenever I heard the word "problem," I would joke that "problem" is a negative word used as an excuse by incapable people. Problems are situations created for the purpose of solving.

I continued to work, establishing Stevens International Graphic Consultants. International was not there for show; two of my clients were large Japanese corporations and one was German. One of the firms offered me a lucrative position in the United States, which I rejected. After I had received numerous phone calls from Japan asking me to reconsider, I was finally able to dissuade them, saying that I was now an old man, who only needed to wear one suit at a time and who thought that eating simple food, and less of it, was healthier. Even so, I became busier than I had been at Amway. Finally, after I started receiving many late-night calls from the night shift at a large Cincinnati company, I cut my activities and slowed down.

But the saddest period of my life came when Mary became gravely ill and died. My own health was affected, and I suffered a stroke. Looking back, my greatest achievement was to have been able to raise, with Mary, a family of whom I am very proud.

Finally, I am still able to greet the day with: "Good morning."

EPILOGUE

ᘒ

For a long time after the war it was difficult to talk about my past. I forced myself to forget, wanting to eliminate from my memory the terrible experiences and gruesome pictures that haunted me. But I could not. I thought about the war when I tried to fall asleep in the evening, when I lay awake during the night, even when I awoke first thing in the morning. Reading in the night, listening to the radio, or watching television didn't help. Whether I was tired or sleepy, nothing worked until I started my daily routine.

Realizing that it was impossible to go through the rest of my life like that, I tried all sorts of remedies. When in bed I tried a sort of meditation, calming myself by thinking about nothing. That helped. I also stopped reading anything that might have reminded me of the war. I refused all requests from various organizations to speak publicly about my history.

Later, when Professor William Baum of Grand Valley State University learned I was a Holocaust survivor, he approached me with a request to share my experiences with his classes at GVSU. Eventually, I agreed. It was not easy at the beginning. I was a little disorganized, and I would talk only about those events that were not painful. I noticed that the students, while attentive, were also amused. Some of the stories I recounted sounded like excerpts from the old television series, *Hogan's Heroes*. That was not what I had intended to convey to them. But the more difficult things would not pass my throat.

After much soul searching I decided to share the facts as I had lived them. But even now, after so many years, I cannot talk or write about some terrible scenes and unbelievable experiences. Over the years I have also been asked to share my story with students at Hope College, Aquinas College, high schools, churches, and other organizations. The most difficult task has been speaking with groups in high schools and middle schools. I would have the feeling that younger students did not understand what I was talking about, that it all seemed unreal to them.

My visits to Professor Baum's classes became more frequent, almost routine. His more mature students are always attentive and serious about the subject matter. Following my talks in these classes are question-and-answer periods which usually exceed the allotted time. The students' questions show that they are familiar with the subject matter. Avoiding generalizations, I base my answers on my own experiences. One unusual question, a personal one, has stuck in my mind. A student asked if, after what I had experienced and what I had seen, I still believed in God. I had to think for a minute before I could answer. I explained that I was born to a Jewish family with a Jewish faith, a monotheistic religion with the Ten Commandments as its foundation. Disregarding the question of how the Law originated, I still believe in the Ten Commandments. I wanted to continue; but in keeping with my rule of avoiding theoretical comment, I stopped.

If I had continued, I would have said something like the following: Historically, most wars and killing have been justified on economic, national, religious, or chauvinistic grounds. Competition among religions, where one claims to be the only legitimate faith has also caused much misery. God is supposed to be merciful. But inquisitions, holy wars, and other horrors advanced in the name of religion, creed, or race have caused millions and millions of innocent people to suffer and die. A single individual can convert or excite people like ourselves into hordes of killers. In my life, Stalin and Hitler, to mention just two, managed to poison the minds of much of Europe.

And the rest of the world stood silent . . .

GLOSSARY

Anschluss (Ger.) .... The annexation of Austria into the German State

Armia Krajowa (Pol.) .... National Army, subordinate to Polish government-in-exile

Armia Ludowa (Pol.) .... People's Army, subordinate to Communist Party

Ausländer (Ger.) .... Foreigner, alien

Aryan (Ger.) .... Of the Aryan "race"

Bescheinigung (Ger.) .... Document

Blitzkrieg (Ger.) .... Lightning war

Breslau (Ger.) .... City in eastern Germany, now Wrocław, a Polish city in Silesia

Bug (Pol.) .... River in eastern Poland

Czarnina (Pol.) .... Sausage made of blood and groats

Fokker (Ger.) .... German air force plane

Heldenplatz (Ger.) .... Heroes' Square in Vienna, Austria

Jude (Ger.) .... Jew

Karlsbad (Ger.) .... Health resort city in Czechoslovakia

Katyń (Pol.) .... Forest where thousands of Polish officers were executed by Russians

Kaunas (Lith.) .... Former capital city of Lithuania

Leipzig (Ger.) .... German industrial city; Lipsk in Polish

Łódź (Pol.) .... City in central Poland, renamed Litzmannstadt by the Germans

Lublin (Pol.) .... City in eastern Poland

Łuck (Pol.) .... City in southeastern Poland

Luftwaffe (Ger.) .... German Air Force

Okęcie (Pol.) .... Airport near Warsaw; also, Polish army air base

---

238

Oświęcim (Pol.) .... Auschwitz (Ger.), the largest German extermination camp in Poland

Ponary (Pol.) .... Mass execution site near Vilnius

Posen (Ger.) .... Western Polish city; Poznań in Polish

Reichsmark (Ger.) .... German currency during World War II

Ruble (Rus.) .... Russian currency

Samogon (Pol.) .... Moonshine

Schnapps (Ger.) .... German alcoholic beverage

Stuka (Ger.) .... German air force dive bomber

Vienna (Eng.) .... Austrian capital city; Wien in German

Vilnius (Lith.) .... Lithuanian capital; formerly Wilno, a Polish city

Volksdeutch (Ger.) .... A foreigner of German extraction

Warsaw (Eng.) .... Polish capital city; Warszawa in Polish

Wehrmacht (Ger.) .... German military forces

Woywoki (Rus.) .... Russian warm woolen boots

Pronunciation Equivalents

Polish	English
C	Ts
Cz	Ch
J	Y
Rz	Zh
Sz	Sh
Ł	W
W	V

Joseph Stevens was born in Kalisz, Poland. Trained at the Federal Graphic Institute of Learning and Research in Vienna, he worked in his family's printing firm until the outbreak of the Second World War. He and his wife, Mary, moved to the United States in 1949, where Stevens began working for the National Lithographic Company in Detroit. Seven years later he started his first business in Grand Rapids, National Correct Color Service. Citing his efforts as a Holocaust witness for the West Michigan community, Grand Valley State University created the Joseph Stevens Freedom Endowment in his honor.